The Hidden Power
of the Believer's Touch

The Hidden Power of the Believer's Touch

Mahesh Chavda

Destiny Image® Publishers, Inc.
P.O. Box 310
Shippensburg, PA 17257-0310

"Speaking to the Purposes of God for This Generation
and for the Generations to Come"

ISBN 0-7684-1974-3

For Worldwide Distribution
Printed in the U.S.A.

This book and all other Destiny Image, Revival Press, MercyPlace, Fresh Bread, and Treasure House books are available at Christian bookstores and distributors worldwide.

For a U.S. bookstore nearest you, call **1-800-722-6774**.
For more information on foreign distributors, call **717-532-3040**.
Or reach us on the Internet: **http://www.reapernet.com**

Dedication

This book is lovingly dedicated to our precious Holy Spirit, who makes real every day the healing power of the Lord Jesus Christ.

Acknowledgments

Thanks…

- To my wife, Bonnie—helpmate, friend, and most committed intercessor on our pilgrimage in healing.

- To my four children—Ben, Anna, Serah, and Aaron. You bring delight to my heart.

- To Karen Johnston, my secretary, who has given countless hours of diligent labor to this ministry and contributed much to the completion of this book—bless you for your devotion.

Contents

Introduction

I T IS MY PRAYER that in these pages you will catch a personal glimpse of the Great Physician, and feel the breeze of the healing wind of the Holy Spirit over your life and ministry.

I have sat by the hospital beds of my four children under the most painful circumstances. Of my two sons, the doctors basically acknowledged that they were dying, and that they could do little to help. I heard my daughter's screams of pain after a terrible accident. Only another parent can understand the heartache in these moments. And yet...And yet...

I saw the power of the healing touch in each of these circumstances and hundreds more. Today, my children are strong and healthy, growing daily in the grace of God. There is an English idiom, "The proof of the pudding is in the eating." The principles shared here are real. They work. When I now embrace my grown, healthy children, I am so grateful. I know that I owe it all to the grace of Christ and the power of the believer's healing touch. A believer is simply any person who has put his faith in Jesus Christ. If you are a believer, according to Mark 16:15, signs will follow you.

I am not so much interested in proving theological points in this book. It is more a manual of instruction and inspiration for those hungry to see more of the reality and power of God flow in their lives. Herein you will find the fruit of my pains, struggles, and triumphs. You may be a person who wants to help meet needs in your own life or in those of your family or friends. There are also those of you who have been touched by the river of God's Holy Spirit. You know this fresh anointing is molding you for your destiny and calling. This book is for you. May you be used to touch the needs of a hurting world.

In the following chapters I share lessons and principles molded in the fire over a track record of 25 years of moving under a healing mantle. We have hundreds of testimonies of wonderful healings on file. I want to say that it works, it works!

As you read on, it is my prayer that the King of Glory will give you instruction, inspiration, and a fresh anointing to do exploits before the second coming of Christ. May you fulfill Christ's promise to the one who would believe on Him, "The works that I do he will do also; and greater works than these he will do" (Jn. 14:12).

Once you have finished reading, start putting it into practice. And remember, the Lord gets all the glory for every victory. Luke 13:13, "He laid His hands on her, and immediately she was made straight, and glorified God."

Part One

Understanding the Healing Anointing

Chapter One

The Lord Our Healer

As soon as the call came from the hospital, I knew immediately that something was terribly wrong. Just a few days earlier, my wife, Bonnie, had given birth to Benjamin, our firstborn. As a new father, I was so proud. I had a *son*! Bonnie and I had waited a long time for this exciting day, and I was eagerly looking forward to bringing both of them home. Now, however, the hospital would not release Benjamin. Instead, they had summoned me to the intensive care unit. My mind raced. *What's the matter? What's gone wrong?*

When I walked into the ICU, one of my worst fears was realized. Our doctor and five specialists met me with the news; Benjamin was in trouble. A routine examination had revealed a serious problem. "At first, I thought it was a cancerous tumor," our doctor said, "but it is worse than that—far worse. Your son has a congenital birth defect in his kidneys. Most of both kidneys were destroyed while he was still in the womb."

He then referred us to a special children's hospital in Miami, where specialists performed several surgeries on tiny Benjamin in an effort to correct the problem. They injected radioactive dye into his kidneys and took x-rays to track the path of the dye through his system. The x-rays clearly revealed that most of Benjamin's kidney cells were dead. Bonnie and I were advised to prepare for the worst. We were told that Benjamin

3

would die within a few weeks or, at most, a few months because the infection would kill the rest of his kidney cells.

We were not willing or prepared to accept this outcome. During those days and weeks while Benjamin clung precariously to life, the Holy Spirit led me through a faith-building exercise. I fasted and prayed for my son. I searched the Scriptures for all the verses on healing I could find and wrote them down, inserting my son's name into them. Then I claimed those healing promises specifically for my son. "By His stripes my son Benjamin is healed. God is sending His Word and healing my son Benjamin." I did this day after day, writing out and claiming Scriptures, meditating, and praying.

For a while it seemed as though nothing was happening. When he was three months old, Benjamin underwent a final round of surgery that lasted six hours but accomplished little. The doctors had done everything they could do and advised us, "Pray, for we cannot give him new kidneys." Benjamin came out of surgery with tubes in his side, in his bladder, and in his kidneys. He was screaming in pain. The nurses began crying and said, "We are sorry, but we cannot give Benjamin any pain medication because it would stop his heart."

Benjamin was taken to a special room where he was hooked up to electronic equipment that continuously monitored his vital signs. We were told that he would be in constant pain. Every time Benjamin screamed, the signal on the television monitor would rise and fall, registering the trauma to his tiny body and the intensity of his pain. The nurses, still crying for Benjamin and their inability to ease his suffering, would not let us stay there. "Come back in a few hours and we will let you see him."

Most of you, particularly you parents, can imagine how we felt. Every tormented scream from our infant son stabbed through us like a knife! We wanted so much to be able to scoop him up in our arms, to hug and kiss and soothe and love away the hurt. Our son was slowly dying in excruciating pain—and we felt so helpless.

I remember going outside that day and praying, "Lord, I have shared Your Word around the world; I have seen countless numbers of people brought to Christ; I have witnessed signs and wonders and miracles of

4

healing by the thousands; now I need to experience this *personally*. For myself and for my family, I need to *know* that Jesus took our pain and our infirmity and that 'by His stripes we are healed.'"[1]

When we were allowed into Benjamin's special room several hours later, the nurse, with tears still in her eyes, said, "Something is happening."

My heart sank. "Is he dying?"

"No, sir. Look at the monitor."

The signal on the screen was going up and down just as before. I said, "He is still in great pain."

The nurse replied, "No, sir. I don't understand this, but take a look at your son."

I went behind the screen and looked down at my precious little Benjamin. He was fast asleep and smiling with his arms and hands stretched out. A glowing, golden light surrounded him, and he was beautifully, blissfully at peace. According to the television monitor, he was wracked with spasms of incredible pain. The doctors had described it as similar to the pain of a woman in childbirth. Yet it was obvious that Benjamin felt nothing. That night, at that moment, in a way that I could not understand, I realized that Jesus had taken away his pain. As never before, I was learning the truth that "by His stripes we are healed." Somehow, Benjamin had gotten plugged into the power of God—the experience of Calvary two thousand years ago. God was healing my son!

A few days later a new set of x-rays revealed that Benjamin's kidneys were alive and completely restored! The doctors were at a loss to explain it. They speculated that perhaps somehow the earlier x-rays had been in error, but I knew what had happened. Jesus had taken away my son's pain and God had literally recreated his kidneys!

The Source of All Healing

B ENJAMIN'S HEALING ILLUSTRATES several important things that I want to emphasize at the outset of this book. First, *I believe in doctors and in the science and practice of modern medicine*. No matter where I minister in this country or in other parts of the world, and no matter how many people come forward for healing prayer, I always encourage them to seek out whatever good quality medical care is available to them. Normally, I would never advise anyone to forsake legitimate medical treatment. Medicine and the healing arts are gifts from God, part of His divine and merciful provision for alleviating human suffering. I commend the countless physicians, nurses, medical researchers and scientists, and all other members of the health care profession around the world who dedicate their lives daily to eradicating disease and treating the sick and injured.

Having said that, it is crucial to recognize secondly that *modern medicine has its limits*. Despite the giant leaps forward in medical knowledge and treatment, particularly during the twentieth century, there are hundreds of diseases and conditions that continue to elude a final cure. Cancer, heart disease, and AIDS are only three examples. The medical specialists at the children's hospital in Miami reached the point where they could do nothing more for Benjamin. His condition was beyond their knowledge and skill. Modern medicine simply does not have all the answers. Not only that, but due to political, economic, cultural, and even religious factors, much of the advanced medical care that exists today is not available equally to everyone in the world.

Thirdly, Benjamin's healing shows us that *God can do what even modern medicine cannot do*. God has *always* been in the healing business. The Scriptures, both Old and New Testaments, are full of examples. Accounts of miraculous divine healings are found also throughout Church history. It is no different today in our advanced, scientific, and sophisticated day and age. Divine healing has been a regular and common occurrence for years at my meetings and crusades as God has sovereignly and graciously poured out His healing anointing.

Once, a lady named Kathy from Chicago came forward for prayer. "My mother is dying of pancreatic cancer," she told me. Today, pancreatic cancer is one of the least known and least understood forms of cancer. It is also an extremely aggressive cancer. Because so little is known about it, in most cases those who are diagnosed with pancreatic cancer have a very poor prognosis for recovery. It is just like being issued a death warrant. In this instance, the doctors had given the mother a month to live *at most*. I prayed over this daughter who stood *in proxy* for her mother. The daughter got under the healing anointing, and the Lord reached out to her mother, who was miles away, and *completely healed her of her pancreatic cancer!* God still heals today!

With that, we arrive at the most important truth of all. *Ultimately, God is the source of all healing*, whether it comes through the "miracle" of modern medicine or the miracle of divine intervention. In the 15th chapter of Exodus, Moses and the Israelites sing a song of celebration for God's deliverance at the Red Sea and for His triumph over the army of the pharaoh. Following the song, Moses leads the people three days into the wilderness to a place called Marah,[2] where the only water they can find is too bitter to drink. When the people complain, Moses cries out to God. At the Lord's direction, Moses casts a certain tree into the water, which then becomes sweet.[3]

> *There He made a statute and an ordinance for them, and there He tested them, and said, "If you diligently heed the voice of the Lord your God and do what is right in His sight, give ear to His commandments and keep all His statutes, I will put none of the diseases on you which I have brought on the Egyptians. For I am the Lord who heals you.[4]*

"I am the Lord who heals you." That's pretty clear, isn't it? King David stated it just as clearly in Psalm 103:

> *Bless the Lord, O my soul;*
> *And all that is within me, bless His holy name!*
> *Bless the Lord, O my soul,*
> *And forget not all His benefits:*
> *Who forgives all your iniquities,*
> *Who heals all your diseases.[5]*

There is much more in both of these passages than just healing, but the point I want to make here is that these Scriptures (and many others)[6] clearly indicate that *God is the source of healing*. Ultimately, all healing flows from Him.

Greater Works Than These

HEALING THE SICK was a regular and common part of Jesus' public ministry. It was both an evidence of the truth and power of the message He preached and an expression of God's love and compassion for hurting humanity. Everywhere He went, people flocked to Him, bringing the sick, the lame, and the demon-possessed. Jesus preached and taught that the Kingdom of God was at hand. Then He demonstrated its presence by healing the sick in the power of the Holy Spirit, by feeding the hungry, or by casting out demons.

One Sabbath, while visiting His hometown of Nazareth, Jesus went into the synagogue. As a "hometown boy" and visiting rabbi, He was invited to read the Scripture. The passage for that day, from the prophet Isaiah, expressed the very heart and soul of Jesus' ministry.

> *The Spirit of the Lord is upon Me,*
> *Because He has anointed Me*
> *To preach the gospel to the poor;*
> *He has sent Me to heal the brokenhearted,*
> *To proclaim liberty to the captives*
> *And recovery of sight to the blind,*
> *To set at liberty those who are oppressed;*
> *To proclaim the acceptable year of the Lord.*[7]

The Spirit of God *anointed* Jesus to preach good news to the poor and proclaim liberty to the captives. That heavenly anointing *also* included *healing* the brokenhearted, *restoring sight* to the blind, and *liberating the oppressed*. Jesus' mission was to preach the Word of God *and* to perform signs and wonders as evidence of the truth of His message. His final, signature act was to die on the cross as the Lamb of God, the once-for-all atoning sacrifice for the sins of humanity. The same Spirit who had anointed Jesus and empowered His ministry raised Him from the dead three days later.

8

In light of all the wondrous things Jesus did, one of the most shocking, mind-boggling things He ever said was a promise He made to His disciples the night before His death. It is a key statement to understanding this book and to understanding how the healing anointing relates to us today.

> *Most assuredly, I say to you, he who believes in Me, the works that I do he will do also; and greater works than these he will do, because I go to My Father. And whatever you ask in My name, that I will do, that the Father may be glorified in the Son. If you ask anything in My name, I will do it.*[8]

What are the "works" and the "greater works" that Jesus spoke of here? The answer to that question has been debated for generations. How we answer it today often defines where we stand with regard to expecting the miraculous in our own generation. If we understand Jesus' mission as involving both preaching the Word and performing signs and wonders, then it is logical and reasonable to understand that His "works" include both. In the New Testament, healings, signs, and wonders were all part of the total gospel package—the "full gospel"—that was preached not only by Jesus but also by the apostles and other first-century believers.

Indeed, Jesus' followers *did* do the works that He did—the Book of Acts is ample proof of that—but how could anyone do "greater works" than Jesus Christ? When we talk about "greater" works, we must mean either greater in quantity or scope, or greater in quality. Is it possible for *anyone* to exceed the *quality* of Jesus' works? I don't think so. Exceeding them in quantity and scope is another matter. Jesus' work was limited by time and geography to a few short years and a few hundred square miles (at most); the Church has had centuries, with the entire world as its scope. Through the ages Jesus' followers have reached and touched more people than Jesus ever did directly. The "works" that Christ has performed *through* His people, including signs and wonders, have far surpassed in *quantity* and *scope* the works that Jesus Himself did during His earthly ministry.

Jesus' promise is open-ended; the "works" and the "greater works" are for "he who believes in Me." That includes you and me. Jesus did the works that He did because the anointing of the Spirit of God was upon Him. He has given that same anointing to all His followers through the Holy Spirit who indwells every believer. The anointing of the Spirit— including the healing anointing—is for *all* of us.

The Lord Never Changes

ONE OF THE GREAT AND ENCOURAGING ASSERTIONS of Scripture is that God never changes; He is always the same, day in and day out, from generation to generation. That which was true of God yesterday is true of Him today and will be true of Him tomorrow. Both the Old and New Testaments plainly state this truth: "For I am the Lord, I do not change'"; "Every good gift and every perfect gift is from above, and comes down from the Father of lights, with whom there is no variation or shadow of turning"[10]; "Jesus Christ is the same yesterday, today, and forever."[11]

Two thousand years ago, Jesus saved from their sins all who turned to Him in repentance and faith; He is *still* saving sinners two thousand years later! Two thousand years ago, Jesus healed the sick; He is *still* healing the sick two thousand years later!

In October 1989, I held a healing service at the Hilton Hotel in Jerusalem. During that service a woman named Miriam[12] came forward to receive prayer. A Palestinian Arab who was also a Christian, Miriam had cancerous tumors in both breasts and had been under radiation therapy for ten years. Her condition was such that she frequently suffered from bleeding from both breasts. This bleeding occurred even during the healing service itself. At the time of this meeting, she was scheduled to have a radical mastectomy the following January. In addition to her condition, Miriam's husband suffered from a respiratory problem that made it very difficult for him to breathe.

Although she was a Christian, Miriam did not believe in divine healing for today. She had come to the meeting at the invitation of some Christian friends from America. When the prayer time came, Miriam's friends encouraged her to receive prayer in spite of her unbelief. She went forward to stand in proxy for her husband, that he might be healed of his respiratory problem. Miriam was slain in the Spirit and lay unconscious for *three hours*! During that time, hot water began to flow from

10

her breasts in such quantity that when she finally got up, she had to wring the water from the hem of her dress! For Miriam, this was a sign from the Lord that He had healed her. She went home that night to find that her husband had also been healed.

A short time later, Miriam reported to her Jewish doctor for a pre-surgery examination, which included x-rays. The x-rays showed *no trace of cancer*! Miriam's doctor acted angry with her at first, demanding to know what other doctor she had seen for treatment, and why she hadn't told him about it. Miriam said, "I went to the best doctor in the world—the Lord Jesus Christ!" Then she shared with him how she had received prayer for healing. The doctor replied, "I have heard of this happening in the United States, but never in Israel. You are completely healed."

A year later I returned to Israel for another healing service. Miriam was there again, this time completely well and healthy. No surgery of any kind had been necessary. At that service Miriam presented two sets of x-rays and doctor's reports. The first set confirmed the presence of cancer and prescribed surgery; the second set confirmed that no cancer was present and gave her a clean bill of health.

There is something else that I find very interesting about Miriam's story—she was from the village of Nazareth, Jesus' hometown! Two thousand years after He died, rose again, and ascended into Heaven, Jesus Christ, the Great Physician—the carpenter from Nazareth—reached down and healed a modern-day "daughter" of Nazareth. Jesus Christ is the same yesterday, today, and forever!

These Signs Will Follow

BEFORE HE ASCENDED TO HEAVEN after His resurrection, Jesus issued marching orders to His disciples. He charged them with a commission that applied not only to them but also to every believer of every generation who would follow, including us. The Great Commission of Matthew 28:18-20 is the most familiar version, but for our purposes in this book I want to look at the version found in the Gospel of Mark.

> *And He said to them, "Go into all the world and preach the gospel to every creature. He who believes and is baptized will*

be saved; but he who does not believe will be condemned. And these signs will follow those who believe: In My name they will cast out demons; they will speak with new tongues; they will take up serpents; and if they drink anything deadly, it will by no means hurt them; they will lay hands on the sick, and they will recover."[13]

These are some of the last recorded words of Jesus. Everything Jesus said is important, but His final words have special significance. His instructions enabled His disciples to change the destiny of humanity and shape the future course of history. If the disciples had not hearkened to Jesus' words, you and I would not be here today. Most of us would either be worshiping in mosques as Muslims, or following the ways of some other Eastern religion, such as Hinduism, Buddhism, or Shintoism. It is because of the faithfulness and obedience of that motley crew of disciples that we stand today before the Lord as believers and have the privilege of sharing the good news of Christ with yet another generation.

Jesus' Great Commission in Mark is both a charge to "preach the gospel to every creature," and a promise of "signs" that would follow as divine confirmation of the truth of the gospel message. It is an open-ended promise: The signs will follow *those who believe*. That means you and me. This does not mean that we have a free license to test the Lord by deliberately practicing dangerous acts such as handling venomous snakes or drinking poison. It *does* mean that He will empower us to fulfill His will and purpose and will verify the truth of the gospel we preach with attesting signs and wonders.

Yet, many modern Christians, particularly in the West, insist that healings, signs, and wonders are not for today. They were important for helping to establish the gospel and the Church in the first century until the full written canon of Scripture was completed, but are now no longer needed. Besides, so the argument goes, aside from the first century, signs and wonders have not been the *normative* experience of the Church throughout history.

Whether or not this is true, nothing in Scripture precludes God from ushering in a new era, a new anointing for signs and wonders. There is nothing in the Word of God to prevent Him from reestablishing conditions similar to those that existed in the first century, particularly as we move ever closer to the end of the age and the consummation of all things. As spiritual darkness increases in the world, so will the divine light of the Spirit shine with ever-growing intensity.

The twentieth century witnessed a definite increase of signs and wonders in the Church as God released a fresh outpouring of His Spirit on His people. Another sign of a "new era" was the rise of healing evangelists, such as Aimee Semple McPherson, Oral Roberts, Kathryn Kuhlman, and others. Today, we are living in an unprecedented age of the Church. God is doing things in our midst that the world has not witnessed for two thousand years. He has planted each of us in our particular time and place for a particular purpose. This is *our* generation; this is *our* time to shine for God. Jesus said that we are to "preach the gospel to every creature." One of the signs that will follow is we "will lay hands on the sick, and they will recover." This is *our* time to *flow with the current of the Spirit's anointing*!

Adventures on the River

PSALM 46:4 SAYS, "There is a river whose streams shall make glad the city of God, the holy place of the tabernacle of the Most High." In recent years, multitudes of Christians have been "made glad" by "soaking" in the "river" of God, the fresh outpouring of His Spirit that has sparked new life and new energy to the Church. It feels so good to rest in the anointing, to absorb the warmth of the manifold blessings of God! There is nothing quite like the tender, loving touch of the Lord on our hearts. The "river" is wonderful, but we have reached a point where we need to ask ourselves, "What now? Why are we in the river? What is its purpose? Is God interested only in giving His children warm feelings, or does He have something more in mind?"

Every river has a current that carries along whatever is caught in or yielded to its influence. If you are interested in traveling downstream, all you have to do is steer your boat into the current and it will take you there. Along the way you may encounter shallows, eddies, rocks, rapids, or whirlpools; but if you stay in the current, you will eventually reach your destination. Sometimes it is very tempting to let yourself drift off into a side eddy where that water has been separated from the main flow of the river. Away from the current, the water becomes very still. Although you may find it very quiet, peaceful, and relaxing in the eddy, you also are not going anywhere. Sometimes that is good. We all need times to rest and take our bearings. If we want to reach our goal, however, we can't stay in the eddy. Water that stays still too long becomes stagnant—a collection point for twigs, dead leaves, scum, and algae. We must get back into the current. *Life grows where the river flows.*

At 1,286 feet below sea level, the Dead Sea is the lowest point on the face of the earth. This inland lake on the Israeli-Jordanian border is aptly named. The alkali content of the water is so high that almost nothing can live in it. Known also as the Salt Sea, the lake and its surrounding shores have been a source of salt mining since ancient times. The reason the Dead Sea is so brackish is because although it has an inlet, the Jordan River, it has no outlet. The lake receives and receives and receives, but it never gives anything back. Evaporation is the only way water ever leaves the Dead Sea. With nowhere to go, the water stagnates.

A similar danger exists for us as Christians if we get too caught up in simply enjoying the "river" of God for our own sake. If all we do is receive, receive, receive the spiritual "water" of God—His anointing— and never give it out, that water in us will become a stagnant pool. Many times we're willing to venture just far enough into the river to "taste and see that the Lord is good,"[16] but not far enough to let ourselves get swept away by the "current" of His Spirit. We are eager for the anointing but afraid of where it might take us. So we stay close to the bank with one hand gripped tightly to a tree limb, never daring to let go, plunge into the middle of the river, and let the current take us where it will.

This is one of the reasons many Christians that I meet, particularly charismatics, are expressing discouragement with their spiritual journey. They have experienced the joy of receiving the Spirit's anointing, only to have it lift and depart later. These disappointed believers don't know how to keep the anointing by walking in it daily. Many of them do not understand that the anointing is not for *us* as much as it is for *others*. We can't keep the anointing unless we are willing to give it away.

14

I want to invite—no, *challenge*—you to join me for a great adventure on the river. We will be like daring explorers, boldly journeying along the rushing, roiling river of God, sitting squarely in the middle of the current—the Holy Spirit—and allowing Him to take us wherever He will. Where will He take us? The journey that lies before us is the same one that Jesus has already taken:

> *The Spirit of the Lord is upon Me,*
> *Because He has anointed Me*
> *To preach the gospel to the poor;*
> *He has sent Me to heal the brokenhearted,*
> *To proclaim liberty to the captives*
> *And recovery of sight to the blind,*
> *To set at liberty those who are oppressed;*
> *To proclaim the acceptable year of the Lord.*[15]

Success on our river journey depends on our learning how to "flow with the current" in order to reach the Lord's desired destination for us. As we learn to "flow" with the anointing, He will take us where He wants us to go: to the poor, the sick, the hurting, and the lost. Along the way we will learn that every believer can walk in the healing anointing of the Lord. God wants to use His people—*us*—to bring healing (both physical and spiritual) to the nations.

Jesus healed and accomplished all His other works under the power of the anointing of God's Spirit. In his Gospel, Luke wrote of Jesus that "on a certain day…the power of the Lord was present to heal…."[16] Jesus focused on the anointing of the Spirit as He said and did everything He had received from His Father. We too must focus on the anointing, not for its own sake, or for ourselves, but in order to fulfill the purpose of God in our lives. He has given us the anointing for a reason, and that reason is as big and as broad as the world itself. The only way we can understand it and fulfill it is to plunge into the river.

Are you ready to get wet? *Then let the adventure begin!*

Endnotes

1. Is. 53:5b.

2. *Marah* literally means "bitter."

3. See Ex. 15:22-25.

4. Ex. 15:25b-26.

5. Ps. 103:1-3.

6. For example, see Gen. 20:17; Deut. 32:39; 2 Kings 5:1-15; 20:1-11; 2 Chron. 7:14; Ps. 30:2; 107:20; 147:3; Is. 53:5; 57:19; 61:1-3; Jer. 17:14; 30:17; Ezek. 47:1-9; Hos. 6:1; Mt. 4:24; 8:5-13,16; 9:18-26; 10:1; 12:15,22; 14:14; 15:28,30; 19:2; 21:14; Mk. 1:34; 3:10; 5:21-43; 6:5,13; Lk. 4:18,40; 5:17-26; 6:17-19; 7:1-10; 8:26-56; 9:1-2,11; Jn. 5:1-9; Acts 3:1-16; 4:24-31; 5:12-16; 8:4-8; 9:32-35; 28:8-9; 1 Pet. 2:24.

7. Lk. 4:18-19.

8. Jn. 14:12-14.

9. Mal. 3:6a.

10. Jas. 1:17.

11. Heb. 13:8.

12. "Miriam" is not her real name. Because of her "political" position as a Palestinian Arab who loves the Jews and supports the state of Israel, I have concealed her identity to protect her and her family.

13. Mk. 16:15-18.

14. Ps. 34:8a.

15. Lk. 4:18.

16. Lk. 5:17.

Chapter Two

The Power of the Gospel

EVERY RIVER HAS A SOURCE, a place of beginning where it rises from a lake or a spring or a mountain stream. America's largest and mightiest river, the Mississippi, begins as a small stream flowing from Lake Itasca in Minnesota.[1] South America's Amazon River, the second-longest river in the world, has its source high in the Andes Mountains of Peru, less than 100 miles from the Pacific Ocean. By the time it empties into the Atlantic Ocean, almost 4000 miles later, it has become the most powerful watercourse in the world, carrying as much as 20 percent of all the water that drains off the earth's surface. The Amazon's discharge at its mouth is "so great that it turns seawater from salty to brackish for more than 100 miles offshore."[2] Africa's Nile River, which has nourished civilization continuously for over five thousand years, rises in the eastern lakes region of the central African nation of Burundi. It is the longest river in the world, flowing 4,132 miles northward before draining into the Mediterranean Sea north of Cairo, Egypt.[3]

Like the Mississippi, the Amazon, and the Nile, the "river" of God also has a source: the heart of God Himself. Through His Word—both written and incarnate, as personified in His Son, Jesus Christ-and through His Spirit, God has poured out upon humanity the very essence of His Person and character. Just as a river of water issues forth from its source, growing as it goes and nourishing with life all that it touches, so it is with

17

the river of God. Divine love, mercy, grace, healing, and salvation flood from the heart of God in a rushing, ever-growing stream that transforms everyone who plunges into its life-giving flow. The central course of that river is Jesus Christ. He is the ultimate expression of God's heart.

The Heart of the Gospel

PERHAPS NO ONE STATED this truth better than the apostle John when he wrote,

> *In the beginning was the Word, and the Word was with God, and the Word was God. He was in the beginning with God....In Him was life, and the life was the light of men....And the Word became flesh and dwelt among us, and we beheld His glory, the glory as of the only begotten of the Father, full of grace and truth.*[4]

Later on in his Gospel, John recorded these words of Jesus: "I am the bread of life,"[5] and "I am the light of the world."[6] To John, Jesus Himself was the very Word of God and the source of all life. He was both *light* and *life*. As such, Jesus was the focal point of everything that John believed, preached, and taught.

Writing to the Colossians, the apostle Paul spoke of Jesus in similar language:

> *He is the image of the invisible God, the firstborn over all creation. For by Him all things were created that are in heaven and that are on earth, visible and invisible, whether thrones or dominions or principalities or powers. All things were created through Him and for Him. And He is before all things, and in Him all things consist....For it pleased the Father that in Him all the fullness should dwell.*[7]

Paul said that all the fullness of God dwelled in Jesus. Jesus, then, was the fullest and most perfect self-expression of God to men. That is why He once told His questioning disciples, "He who has seen Me has seen the Father."[8]

The heart of God's Word to humanity is the gospel—the "good news"—of Jesus Christ. Jesus is more than just the *heart* of the gospel;

18

He *is* the gospel. John and Paul certainly understood this, as did the other apostles and first-century believers. That's why they were able to impact their world and culture the way they did. John wrote, "That which was from the beginning, which we have heard, which we have seen with our eyes, which we have looked upon, and our hands have handled, concerning the Word of life....that which we have seen and heard we declare to you."[9] The "Word of life" is Jesus. Paul also kept the focus of his message clear and simple. "For I determined not to know anything among you except Jesus Christ and Him crucified."[10]

If we want to understand and learn to walk in the healing anointing, we must first recognize the importance of keeping our focus squarely on the *heart* of the gospel. The heart of the gospel is *not* healing. The heart of the gospel is *not* signs and wonders. The heart of the gospel is not even the anointing of the Holy Spirit. *The heart of the gospel is Jesus Christ.* It is only as we clearly proclaim Christ first and foremost that we will experience signs and wonders following.

Jesus performed signs and wonders. So did Peter, John, Paul, and the rest of the apostles, as well as numerous other first-century believers. Signs and wonders authenticated the truth of the gospel message being preached. Rarely, if ever, did they *produce* faith in unbelievers. By far, signs and wonders occurred most often *where faith was already present.* Mark tells of a visit Jesus made to "His own country" where "He could do no mighty work" because of their unbelief.[11] As Paul wrote to the Romans, "So then faith comes by hearing, and hearing by the word of God."[12] Faith does not come by healing, nor does it come by signs and wonders. *Faith comes by hearing the Word of God.* The greatest key to spiritual power in our preaching, teaching, healing, and other ministries is to focus on the gospel. There is great power in the simple message of "Jesus Christ and Him crucified."

There Is Power in the Gospel of Jesus Christ

ONCE, WHEN I WAS IN ZAIRE, the Lord impressed on me the power of the gospel in a very vivid way. We rented an airplane from Mission Aviation Fellowship and flew over hundreds of miles of African terrain to the city of Kikwit. As I looked down, I saw thousands of people coming from villages in every direction, making their way through the jungle toward our meeting place. Many of them had walked as long as seven days to get there. I suddenly realized that, for many of these people, this would be their first and possibly only opportunity to hear the gospel. What should I share with them? What do you say to people who are hearing the gospel for the first time and may never hear it again? The Lord laid on my heart to proclaim the simple good news of Jesus: how He took our sins upon Himself, how He died on Calvary, how He was buried, and how He rose again on the third day.

Beginning with the very first night, spiritually hungry people came by the thousands. As I preached the Word of God—the simple message of Jesus—some of the most awesome things began happening right before our eyes. A 44-year-old man named Kifuala ran up while I was preaching. Kifuala had been a leper for 14 years, and God had healed him completely right there during the service. He had run forward to show everyone that God had cleansed him. Instantly, 14 years of leprosy had left him because *there is power in the gospel of the Lord Jesus Christ!*

Another man was there who had split his leg wide open with an axe while working in the bush. The huge, festering cut was plainly visible on his leg. That night, in front of hundreds of witnesses, the Lord closed and completely healed that cut, leaving no trace of it—not even a scar. *There is power in the gospel of the Lord Jesus Christ!*

A woman came with her three-year-old daughter, who had been born without eyes. At one point during the meeting, we suddenly heard screams. *What's happening?* I wondered. Then the woman ran forward with her daughter. Excitedly she said, "Look at my daughter!" God had come sovereignly and put eyes in the child's empty sockets!

At that time we lost control of the crowd. They tore through all the restraints and tried to grab hold of us, to tear some part of our clothing, to have some kind of physical contact with us. I found myself suddenly surrounded by a ring of tall Africans who, in order to protect me, lifted me over the crowd, put me in a car, locked it, and got me away from there. It wasn't because the crowd was angry or afraid; they were *excited*! They had seen a glimpse of the power of God and they wanted more. *There is power in the gospel of the Lord Jesus Christ!*

God said that His Word would not return to Him void, but would prosper and accomplish everything He desired. [13] Jesus entrusted the keeping and proclaiming of that Word to His disciples and to every other believer in every generation. That includes you and me. We are stewards of the greatest message, the greatest truth in human history, that God "loved us and sent His Son to be the propitiation for our sins."[14]

Sometimes we are tempted to feel that the simple message of Jesus is "old hat" to us, and we get restless for something more. We go from place to place saying, "Give me something new; I want a deeper teaching." Growth and maturity in our faith is certainly desirable and proper, but we need to be careful that in the process we never get tired of the simple gospel of the Lord Jesus. Hidden within the simplicity of the gospel message is the power to save the world. The apostle Paul testified, "For I am not ashamed of the gospel of Christ, for it is the power of God to salvation for everyone who believes, for the Jew first and also for the Greek."[15]

We should never be ashamed or embarrassed by the gospel message that we proclaim. There is no reason for us to be apologetic in claiming that we have the greatest news that anyone has ever heard. When some-one hears the message and understands who Jesus is and what He has done, the way is open for the Holy Spirit to create faith in that person's heart. Remember that faith comes by hearing, and hearing by the Word of God. The moment someone receives the gospel, his eternal destiny is changed. A great transformation takes place. A sinner bound for hell is changed into a citizen of Heaven—a child of the King and an heir to the Kingdom of God. Heaven is his home; God is his Father; and Jesus is his Savior, his Lord, and his elder Brother. No power on earth can bring about such a change. Only God can do it. *There is power in the gospel of the Lord Jesus Christ!*

Simple Acts of Faith Release the Miracles of God

I BELIEVE IT IS SIMPLE ACTS OF FAITH that release the miracles of God. It is not complicated. The more we approach God with childlike faith, the more the doors are opened for us to receive miracles. Jesus said that faith the size of a mustard seed is enough to move a mountain.[16] A woman who had suffered with severe bleeding for 12 years simply touched the hem of Jesus' robe and was completely healed. Jesus told her it was her faith that had made her well.[17]

In the 21st chapter of Numbers the Israelites complained against God and against Moses because they were tired of the wilderness and of the manna they had to eat day after day. In judgment, God sent "fiery serpents" into the camp to bite the people, many of whom died. When the Israelites repented of their sin and cried out for help, God provided relief. "Then the Lord said to Moses, 'Make a fiery serpent, and set it on a pole; and it shall be that everyone who is bitten, when he looks at it, shall live.' So Moses made a bronze serpent, and put it on a pole; and so it was, if a serpent had bitten anyone, when he looked at the bronze serpent, he lived."[18] Any stricken Israelite who exercised simple faith by looking at the bronze serpent was saved from death by snakebite.

Centuries later, Jesus likened the bronze serpent in the wilderness to His own mission.

And as Moses lifted up the serpent in the wilderness, even so must the Son of Man be lifted up, that whoever believes in Him should not perish but have eternal life. For God so loved the world that He gave His only begotten Son, that whoever believes in Him should not perish but have everlasting life. For God did not send His Son into the world to condemn the world, but that the world through Him might be saved.[19]

Just as the Israelites who looked in faith at the bronze serpent lifted up in the wilderness were saved from the bite of the real serpents, so anyone who looks in faith upon Jesus "lifted up" on the cross will be saved from sin—the "bite" of that "serpent," satan. And just as those who looked on the bronze serpent received physical healing, so also the salvation that Jesus provides includes a physical element. We have already seen how the "full gospel" proclaimed by Jesus and His disciples manifested signs and wonders, including physical healing. To be sure, the salvation we receive from Jesus is first and foremost spiritual in nature, cleansing us from sin and restoring us to a right relationship with God. Unfortunately, too many Christians stop right there and never press in to realize the physical aspect of the truth that "by His stripes we are healed."

The foundation for this truth is the love of God. Verse 16 of this passage from the third chapter of John has been called, "the gospel in a nutshell." God's love for sinful humanity prompted Him to send His sinless Son to die for our sins that we might have eternal life by believing in the name of Jesus. This is the scriptural foundation for everything we believe and experience as Christians, whether it is spiritual regeneration or physical healing.

A simple act of faith can release the healing power of God. The apostle Paul healed a man crippled from birth because Paul saw that the man "had faith to be healed." [20] Once, during a meeting in Texas, a mail carrier who was in attendance was completely healed of a severe back injury. For three years he had endured pain so excruciating that no medication he tried had worked. Finally, his doctors had equipped him with a battery to wear that numbed the pain with jolts of electricity.

As he sat in the meeting, and as I said, "Holy Spirit, come," he felt a sudden tingling like an electrical current go through his entire body. Even though he was not completely healed at that moment, he had the faith to know that God was doing something. He stood up to come to the front, but before he got there the Spirit of God came upon him so strongly that he fell down. When he got up again a few minutes later, he took the battery off. For the first time in at least three years he was able to bend over and touch his toes without pain, and the very next day he went out and ran three miles. He came to the meeting the next night and testified that God had completely healed him. He "had faith to be healed," and God honored his faith.

The basis for his healing is found in John 3:16: God loved us so much that He gave us His Son. As we recognize this truth, great power is released in our lives.

Simple Facts of the Gospel

IF SOMEONE CAME UP TO YOU AND ASKED, "What is the gospel?" what would you tell them? How would you explain it? Be careful about your answer, because it is very easy to overcomplicate the gospel. We can get caught up in emotionalism or side issues and lose sight of the basic core message. The gospel consists of a few definite, simple facts, and salvation consists of knowing, believing, and responding to these facts. It is on the basis of these facts that the love, acceptance, and power of God are released in our lives.

So what are the basic, simple facts of the gospel? Let's let the apostle Paul state them for us.

> *...It shall be imputed to us who believe in Him who raised up Jesus our Lord from the dead, who was delivered up because of our offenses, and was raised because of our justification.*[21]

> *Moreover, brethren, I declare to you the gospel which I preached to you, which also you received and in which you stand....For I delivered to you first of all that which I also received: that Christ died for our sins according to the Scriptures, and that He was buried, and that He rose again the third day according to the Scriptures.*[22]

In these two passages from Romans 4 and First Corinthians 15, Paul makes four basic statements about the gospel:

1. Christ died for our sins according to the Scriptures. (He was delivered up because of our offenses.)

2. Christ was buried.

3. Christ rose again the third day according to the Scriptures.

4. Christ was raised from the dead so that we might be justified—made right with God, "just as if" we had never sinned. We are justified (saved) before God when in faith we believe this record of Christ's death, burial, and resurrection on our behalf, and trust Him as our Savior and Lord.

Paul emphasizes two things with regard to these statements. First, if the gospel is to make a difference in our lives, we must *receive* it and we must *stand* in it. As we learn to stand *in* the gospel, we will begin to appropriate the blessings and the power *of* the gospel.

24

Secondly, Paul stresses the authority of the Scriptures over the authority of eyewitnesses as our primary reason for believing and standing in the gospel. He said that Christ died and rose again "according to the Scriptures." In Paul's day, the Scriptures consisted of what we know as the Old Testament. Centuries ahead of time, the prophets of old had foreseen and prophesied the events of Christ's life, death, burial, and resurrection. Later on, Paul would mention the testimony of eyewitnesses as *supporting* the testimony of Scripture, but Scripture always holds the predominant place.

The Word of God is the foundation upon which we stand. We do not stand on circumstance. We do not stand on experience. *We stand on the Word of God.* The Word of God is greater than either our circumstances or our individual experiences. Our circumstances and experiences must be measured against the standard of God's Word. Jesus said, "Heaven and earth will pass away, but My words will by no means pass away."[23] Our salvation and eternal destiny are based on something that will outlast our circumstances, our experiences, and even the natural world itself: the Word of God. *We stand on the Word of God.*

Mind Faith or Heart Faith?

NO MATTER HOW SIMPLE THE GOSPEL IS, it can do us no good until we respond to it in faith. Salvation depends on whether our faith is mind faith or heart faith. There is a big difference. Mind faith is nothing more than an intellectual acceptance of facts. It is passive, requiring neither a supernatural experience nor a change of lifestyle. Heart faith is active faith—faith that we are willing to stake our lives on. Heart faith changes us from the inside out. More than mere acceptance of the facts of the gospel, heart faith creates in us a willingness to respond to and act on those facts. It is the only appropriate response to the gospel message.

The gospel of Christ demands a personal response from each of us. By its very nature, heart faith is deeply and distinctly personal. The Bible describes heart faith in several different ways.

If you confess with your mouth the Lord Jesus and believe in your heart that God has raised Him from the dead, you will be

25

saved. For with the heart one believes unto righteousness, and with the mouth confession is made unto salvation....For "whoever calls on the name of the Lord shall be saved."[24]

Heart faith is confessing Christ with our mouth, believing on Him with our heart, and calling on His name. That means asking God for salvation in the name of Jesus. It means trusting in Him rather than in ourselves or in our own goodness.

Come to Me, all you who labor and are heavy laden, and I will give you rest.[25]

Heart faith means coming willingly to Jesus, giving Him control of our lives. When we do, we find His arms open wide to receive us. But we have to come. It is a deliberate, conscious act of our will. Jesus offers us an open invitation to come and encourages us with a promise: "All that the Father gives Me will come to Me, and the one who comes to Me I will by no means cast out." [26] What a wonderful assurance this is! The invitation is supported by the promise, and the promise creates the required faith in those who desire to accept the invitation.

Sometimes the Bible likens heart faith to quenching our thirst.

If anyone thirsts, let him come to Me and drink. He who believes in Me, as the Scripture has said, out of his heart will flow rivers of living water.[27]

Whoever drinks of the water that I shall give him will never thirst. But the water that I shall give him will become in him a fountain of water springing up into everlasting life.[28]

And the Spirit and the bride say, "Come!" And let him who hears say, "Come!" And let him who thirsts come. Whoever desires, let him take the water of life freely.[29]

The abundant blessings of the Lord are like rivers of living water and He has invited us to drink freely. He cannot drink for us, however, and neither can anyone else. We must each drink personally of Jesus Christ. Mind faith tells us to watch safely from the bank. Heart faith prompts us to plunge into the river.

Probably the most familiar biblical image of heart faith is that of a new birth.

Jesus answered and said to him, "Most assuredly, I say to you, unless one is born again, he cannot see the kingdom of God....Most assuredly, I say to you, unless one is born of water and the Spirit, he cannot enter the kingdom of God. That which is born of the flesh is flesh, and that which is born of the Spirit is spirit. Do not marvel that I said to you, 'You must be born again.' "[30]

When we are truly born again, we will see the Kingdom of God! Our priorities will change. Our greatest desire will be to serve and honor our risen Savior. We will acknowledge Him as the supreme Lord of our life because He bought our salvation with the price of His own blood.

God's Precious Pearl

I ONCE HEARD A TRUE STORY about a man who was browsing at a flea market in Arizona. On one table were several piles of ordinary-looking rocks, with each pile labeled for sale at a low price. One particular pile of these nondescript rocks caught the man's eye, and he bought it for just a few dollars.

To the other people at the flea market it was just a stack of rocks. To the experienced eye of this man, however, it was much more. An expert jeweler, he had seen something that no one else had seen. Hidden in the midst of those ordinary stones was a precious emerald. One of the most perfect emeralds ever found in America, it proved to be worth several million dollars—and he had bought it for almost nothing.

Jesus told two parables that are similar to this story. In the first, a man finds a great treasure buried in a common field; in the second, a merchant discovers a precious pearl. The main difference in these stories is that while the jeweler paid almost nothing for his emerald, the men in Jesus' stories paid everything they had in order to purchase something of supreme value.

Again, the kingdom of heaven is like treasure hidden in a field, which a man found and hid; and for joy over it he goes and sells all that he has and buys that field. Again, the kingdom of heaven is like a merchant seeking beautiful pearls, who, when he had found one pearl of great price, went and sold all that he had and bought it.[31]

Most of us are familiar with these parables as describing the all-surpassing value of the kingdom of Heaven for those who find it. I want to look at these stories from a slightly different angle. In the first parable, the man who finds the treasure is Jesus Christ Himself. The field represents the world, and the treasure is God's people in the world. In the parable, what does the man want? The field or the treasure? He wants the treasure, but to get it he has to buy the field. Even though the price is high—"all that he has"—he pays it joyfully because he recognizes the supreme value of the treasure.

Jesus gave up everything He had, including His very life, to "buy" humanity back from sin. Many people will reject Him and refuse to follow Him, but all those who receive Him become the "treasure" that fills Him with such joy. He paid the price because He wanted a people for Himself. Jesus "gave Himself for us, that He might redeem us from every lawless deed and purify for Himself His own special people, zealous for good works."[32]

Jesus Himself said it this way: "For God so loved the world that He gave His only begotten Son, that whoever believes in Him should not perish but have everlasting life." [33] God sent His Son; what does He get in return? He gets the "whoevers": everyone who believes and trusts in Christ. The "treasure" hidden in the field is the total company of believers, all the "whoevers" of God.

In the second parable, the pearl merchant also represents Jesus. This time, however, the image is even more specific and intimate. The object of the merchant's search is not a hoard of treasured items hidden in a field, but a *single pearl* of great price. Once again, obtaining this pearl costs the merchant everything He has. To an outsider it may seem extravagant, but the merchant knows the value of the pearl.

If the treasure in the field represents *all* of God's people, then the pearl stands for each one of us as *individuals*. Jesus did not die for a nameless, faceless crowd; He died for each of us *personally*. That's how much we mean to Him; that's how valuable we are in His eyes. It doesn't matter who we are, where we are from, or what we have done; Jesus still loves us. Even if the world considers us worthless, Jesus considers us of great value—valuable enough to die for. Jesus looks beyond our dirt, our disease, and our sin, and sees a *pearl*. He is saying to us, "I gave everything I had for you, and now you belong to Me. You are Mine, and no one can ever take you away from Me." Each of us, you and me, is *God's precious pearl*! The price of that pearl was the blood of His Son, Jesus Christ, the Lamb of God who takes away the sin of the world.

The Blood of the Lamb

ONCE, WHEN I WAS REFLECTING on the coming of Christ and His birth in a stable in Bethlehem, I asked, "Lord, why a stable?" His answer made perfect sense. "Where else should a Lamb be born?" John the Baptist testified of Jesus, "Behold! The Lamb of God who takes away the sin of the world."[34] Jesus was the fulfillment of everything toward which the Old Testament Jewish sacrificial system pointed. The high priest would sprinkle the blood of the lamb on the altar and on the mercy seat to make atonement for the sins of the people. Their sins were, in a sense, "covered" by the blood. This made it possible for the people to come into the presence of God and receive blessings rather than curses, and life rather than death.

God told the Israelites, "For the life of the flesh is in the blood, and I have given it to you upon the altar to make atonement for your souls; for it is the blood that makes atonement for the soul."[35] The *life* is in the *blood*. Shed blood is absolutely essential for the forgiveness of sin. "Without shedding of blood there is no remission."[36] During the Last Supper, Jesus held up the cup, which represented His blood, and said to His disciples, "Drink from it, all of you. For this is My blood of the new covenant, which is shed for many for the remission of sins."[37] Jesus is the ultimate, once-for-all Lamb of sacrifice, whose shed blood on the cross has provided the complete, final, and eternal atonement for our sins.

Jesus paid the price because He loves us. Just as the man sold everything he had so he could possess the treasure, and the merchant everything he had so he could possess that single pearl of great price, in the same way Jesus gave up everything He had so He could possess us. He laid aside the splendor and glory of Heaven and poured out His blood on earth because He saw us as pearls worth any price.

There is power in the *gospel* of Jesus Christ because there is power in the *blood* of Jesus Christ! That is why Paul told the Corinthians, "For I determined not to know anything among you except Jesus Christ and Him crucified."[38] Paul understood the power of the blood of Jesus! The blood of Christ removes our sin-guilt and brings us into an eternal relationship with God. John described this as "walking in the light." "But if we walk in the light as He is in the light, we have fellowship with one another, and the blood of Jesus Christ His Son cleanses us from all sin."[39]

There is no substitute for the message of "Jesus Christ and Him crucified." The simple but incredible story of the death, burial, and resurrection of Christ has been the light of the nations for two thousand years. Millions have come to know for themselves the truth that "by His stripes we are healed." The power of God to save and to heal is released whenever we preach the blood of Christ.

Healed by His Stripes

A FEW YEARS AGO we had the privilege of holding a big crusade in San Jose, Costa Rica. Publicized weeks in advance, the meetings were a great success. The Spirit and presence of the Lord were evident in great power. Across eight days, 1,200 people responded to the preaching of the gospel and came to saving faith in Christ. These new believers were counseled, given Bibles, and planted into the churches that had sponsored our crusade. There were also many miraculous healings.

Some of those people whom the Lord touched were reached by radio. Our entire crusade was broadcast live all over Costa Rica, and even reached into Panama and Nicaragua, which was still under communist rule at that time. Not even communists could control the airwaves, however, and we received numerous amazing testimonies of Nicaraguans and others who were saved or instantly healed of tumors or other diseases while listening to the Word of God over the radio.

One of these was a woman who showed up on the third night to share her testimony, having traveled eight hours by bus over bumpy roads just to get there. She described what happened.

"I was listening to this man [pointing to me] on the crusade broadcast three days ago. I had a giant tumor the size of a grapefruit growing inside my throat. As I heard this man preaching the Word of God, the tumor started vibrating. While he preached, the tumor shook more and more violently. Suddenly it burst inside my throat lining and came out of my mouth."[40]

Subsequent x-rays revealed absolutely no trace of the tumor! She was completely healed! That's the power of the gospel of Jesus Christ! Faith had come by hearing the Word of God, and her faith had healed her.

Another woman who listened by radio was healed of a brain tumor. She related that as she was listening to the broadcast, she suddenly felt wetness running down her neck. Fearful that she was bleeding to death but afraid to look, she took a towel, pressed it to the spot on her head, and continued listening. When she removed the towel some time later, the entire tumor was gone! She shared her testimony at onc of the later meetings and showed us where the tumor had been. We even got it on video. Faith rose up in her heart as she heard the Word of God, and her faith healed her.

On another night a woman from one of the outlying villages near San Jose came forward for prayer. Obviously very poor, she was wearing shoes that were old and torn, and her clothes were somewhat ragged and tattered. When I put my hand on her head to pray for her, she took my hand and placed it right over her chest. I was embarrassed at first, until I realized that she had a cancer in her breasts. My initial thought was, *I hope no one is taking pictures.* Through an interpreter she told me that it was malignant. This poor woman had cancer but no money for treatment. She needed a miracle.

I stood before the Lord and said, "Oh Lord, here is one of your precious pearls. You paid the price for her, Lord." She kept on pressing my hand in, and I kept on praying. Finally, I moved on because there were still hundreds more to pray for.

A few minutes later my interpreter said, "Look up." Onto the stage walked the poor woman, torn shoes, tattered clothes and all. She took the microphone, pulled her blouse down a little to show everyone, and said, "I had a malignant tumor, and now it's gone." She was telling the truth; the tumor had disappeared completely! Because of her faith, this woman was healed through the power of the gospel of Jesus Christ.

The gospel of Jesus Christ is the central and essential key to learning how to walk in the healing anointing. Jesus Himself endured the "stripes" by which we are healed, both spiritually and physically. That healing power is released when the gospel is preached. The simple message of "Jesus Christ and Him crucified" is the main stream of the river of God, and gives life, authority, and meaning to everything else. The Holy Spirit is the current that directs that stream and drives it on. No one can understand or receive the gospel apart from the Holy Spirit, who opens our eyes and imparts faith. Neither can we walk in the anointing without Him who gives it and administrates it. In order to be effective in our ministry of the gospel and in handling the anointing, we must come to know and welcome the Holy Spirit who works it all in our hearts and lives. We must understand the purpose, promise, and power of Pentecost.

Endnotes

1. "Mississippi River," Encyclopedia Britannica. <http://www.britannica.com/bcom/eb/article/0/0,5716,54310+1+52987,00.html>.

2. "Amazon River," Encyclopedia Britannica. <http://www.britannica.com/bcom/eb/article/2/0,5716,6112+1+6029,00.html>.

3. "Nile River" Encyclopedia Britannica. <http://www.britannica.com/bcom/eb/article/2/0,5716,57252+1+55849,00.html>.

4. Jn. 1:1-2,4,14.

5. Jn. 6:48.

6. Jn. 8:12b.

7. Col. 1:15-17,19.

8. Jn. 14:9b.

9. 1 Jn. 1:1,3a.

10. 1 Cor. 2:2.

11. See Mk. 6:1-6.

12. Rom. 10:17.

13. See Is. 55:11.

14. 1 Jn. 4:10b.

15. Rom. 1:16.

16. See Mt. 17:20.

17. See Mt. 9:20-22.

18. Num. 21:8-9.

19. Jn. 3:14-17.

20. See Acts 14:8-10.

21. Rom. 4:24-25.

22. 1 Cor. 15:1,3-4.

23. Mt. 24:35.

24. Rom. 10:9-10,13.

25. Mt. 11:28.

26. Jn. 6:37.

27. Jn. 7:37b-38.

28. Jn. 4:14.

29. Rev. 22:17.

30. Jn. 3:3,5-7.

31. Mt. 13:44-46.

32. Tit. 2:14.

33. Jn. 3:16.

34. Jn. 1:29b.

35. Lev. 17:11.

36. Heb. 9:22b.

37. Mt. 26:27b-28.

38. 1 Cor. 2:2.

39. 1 Jn. 1:7.

40. Quoted in Mahesh Chavda, *The Hidden Power of Prayer and Fasting* (Shippensburg, PA: Destiny Image Publishers, Inc., 1998), 163.

Chapter Three

The Purpose of Pentecost

R IVERS ARE CHANNELS OF LIFE that refresh, replenish, and nourish the earth. Four rivers marked the boundaries of the Garden of Eden and fed its abundant fruitfulness. From the earliest times, human settlements have naturally grown up alongside rivers or near springs or some other ready source of water.

For over five thousand years the Nile River has nourished and sustained Egyptian civilization and culture. Since ancient times the people who live along the Nile have depended on its annual spring flood for irrigating crops and for depositing tons of fresh, fertile silt to keep the land arable for farming. The river and its narrow floodplain form a thin, green beltway of life bounded by desert on either side. Although the Aswan High Dam now controls the timing and level of the water, the annual flood is still critical for the thriving of life along the river. *Life grows where the river flows.*

It is the same with the "river" of God. Just as the Nile overflows its banks annually, renewing the land and sustaining the people, so does the "river" of God overflow with the life-giving flood of the Holy Spirit. Any who immerse themselves in this flood receive new health and vigor, becoming productive, fruitful, and full of new life. These are the children of God, of whom the psalmist says, "[They] shall be like a tree planted by the rivers of water, that brings forth its fruit in its season, whose leaf also shall not wither; and whatever [they do] shall prosper." [1] Perhaps the most beautiful picture of this divine river and its life-giving properties is John's description in the Book of Revelation.

> *And he showed me a pure river of water of life, clear as crystal, proceeding from the throne of God and of the Lamb. In the middle of its street, and on either side of the river, was the tree of life, which bore twelve fruits, each tree yielding its fruit every month. The leaves of the tree were for the healing of the nations.* [2]

When we plunge into this river of life, we discover that not only does the Spirit of God quench our own thirst, but He also forms us into vessels and channels through whom He flows to quench the thirst of others. This is what Jesus meant when He said, "If anyone thirsts, let him come to Me and drink. He who believes in Me, as the Scripture has said, out of his heart will flow rivers of living water." [3] The water of life must be *in* our hearts before it can flow *out* of our hearts.

In the very next verse, John explains the significance of Jesus' words. "But this He spoke concerning the Spirit, whom those believing in Him would receive; for the Holy Spirit was not yet given, because Jesus was not yet glorified." [4] According to John, the Holy Spirit could not be given until after Jesus was glorified. It was only after Jesus ascended to Heaven that the Spirit could come down. When He did come down, His coming was the culmination of God's promises across centuries of time.

The Promise of Promises

THE WORD OF GOD contains hundreds of promises to His people, but they are all wrapped up in one package called *the* "Promise." Just before He ascended, Jesus instructed His disciples, "Behold, I send the Promise of My Father upon you; but tarry in the city of Jerusalem until you are endued with power from on high." [5] This "Promise" is the Holy Spirit.

> *And being assembled together with them, He commanded them not to depart from Jerusalem, but to wait for the Promise of the*

36

Father, "which," He said, "you have heard from Me; for John truly baptized with water, but you shall be baptized with the Holy Spirit not many days from now....But you shall receive power when the Holy Spirit has come upon you; and you shall be witnesses to Me in Jerusalem, and in all Judea and Samaria, and to the end of the earth."[6]

The coming of the Spirit was foretold far in advance by Hebrew prophets under God's anointing.

For I will pour water on him who is thirsty, and floods on the dry ground; I will pour My Spirit on your descendants, and My blessing on your offspring; they will spring up among the grass like willows by the watercourses.[7]

I will put My Spirit within you and cause you to walk in My statutes, and you will keep My judgments and do them. Then you shall dwell in the land that I gave to your fathers; you shall be My people, and I will be your God.[8]

And it shall come to pass afterward that I will pour out My Spirit on all flesh; your sons and your daughters shall prophesy, your old men shall dream dreams, your young men shall see visions. And also on My menservants and on My maidservants I will pour out My Spirit in those days.[9]

Centuries passed before the appointed day arrived on God's timetable for the fulfillment of these promises. The Father had done His part; He prepared the way and sent His Son. Jesus did His part; He died for our sins, rose from the dead to make salvation available to us, and ascended to Heaven to be our Advocate before the Father. Now it was time for the Spirit to do His part: administer all the things of God to believers, equipping, gifting, and empowering the Church to do the will of God and fulfill the commission of Christ. When the appointed day came, the Spirit came, and He did not delay.

In One Accord

IN OBEDIENCE TO JESUS' FINAL COMMAND, His followers—120 in number—stayed in Jerusalem, praying together, waiting, and watching.

When the Day of Pentecost had fully come, they were all with one accord in one place. And suddenly there came a sound from heaven, as of a rushing mighty wind, and it filled the whole house where they were sitting. Then there appeared to them divided tongues, as of fire, and one sat upon each of them. And they were all filled with the Holy Spirit and began to speak with other tongues, as the Spirit gave them utterance.[10]

When the Day of Pentecost came (ten days after Jesus' ascension), the believers were gathered together in one place. Ten days of worshiping, praying, watching, and waiting together had brought them into "one accord" in mind and spirit. Although these 120 people were almost certainly all Jews, they were from different family backgrounds. Some were wealthy; most were poor. There were merchants, tax collectors, fishermen, and common laborers. Some may even have been slaves. They had different personalities. It was a very diverse group, yet God brought them together in unity, with a common hunger and thirst for the fullness of the presence of God.

It does not matter whether we are white, black, American Indian, Asian Indian, or Oriental. It does not matter whether we are rich, poor, illiterate, or educated. It does not matter what label we wear—Catholic, Episcopalian, Presbyterian, Baptist, Methodist, or Pentecostal. What matters is how hungry we are for the things of God, and how thirsty we are for His presence and His anointing. Hunger and thirst for the things of the Spirit can bring us together in one accord no matter how different we are. Unity in the Spirit is one of the key conditions for bringing down the glory of God.

Wind and Fire From Heaven

THE ORIGINAL PENTECOSTAL EVENT was a Heaven-born experience of both sound and sight. "A sound from heaven, as of a rushing mighty wind...filled the whole house...Then...divided tongues, as of fire...sat upon each of them." The source of the Pentecostal experience was Heaven itself. It was a completely supernatural event unprecedented in history. Heavenly wind blew, fanning the flames of heavenly fire, which ignited everyone in the room. The Promise had arrived.

The Holy Spirit who came that day was a Person who contained within Himself the power to totally transform people from the inside out. "And they were all filled with the Holy Spirit and began to speak with other tongues, as the Spirit gave them utterance." Perhaps no one in that group of believers was changed more thoroughly than the apostle Peter.

Remember Peter? Peter the impulsive, Peter the headstrong, Peter the boastful, Peter of the hot temper—Peter the *coward*. Peter had spent three years with Jesus. He had heard the teachings, he had seen the miracles, and he had proclaimed his faith in Jesus as the promised Messiah. Yet, despite his strong, manly exterior and rough Galilean fisherman ways, and despite all his boasts of loyalty, when the chips were down, Peter denied his Master. Three times he said of Jesus, "I don't know Him." He even let a simple servant girl in the high priest's household intimidate him. Her accusation left Peter quaking in his sandals.[11] Later, after Jesus was condemned to death, Peter ran away and hid, just like the other disciples.

Pentecost changed Peter. In a matter of moments, the Holy Spirit—that "rushing mighty wind"—filled him and transformed him from a fearful, guilt-ridden denier into a fearless evangelist. As a large crowd gathered to witness the spectacle of these believers speaking in "other tongues, as the Spirit gave them utterance," Peter boldly proclaimed the gospel of Christ in the power of the Spirit. Rivers of living water flowed from Peter's heart and engulfed all those who heard his message. As a result, three thousand new believers were added to the ranks of the Church that day. *Life grows where the river flows!*

A Fresh Visitation of Wind and Fire

WHEN THE HOLY SPIRIT CAME at Pentecost, He took up permanent residence on the earth. His "address" is the heart of every Christian believer in the world. Pentecost ushered in a new age in human history. Never before had the Spirit of God actually *dwelled* in the hearts of men.

As critical as the coming of Jesus was for our salvation, His time on earth was temporary. In His Incarnation, Jesus was limited by His human body to a specific time and a specific place. He could not be "with" all His followers all the time or at the same time. Once He died on the cross and rose from the dead, Jesus had to ascend to Heaven to complete the Father's plan of redemption. He could not stay here. The followers He left behind needed someone who could be with them *all* the time in a way Jesus could not.

That is why the Holy Spirit came. As the third Person of the Trinity, the Holy Spirit is not bound by time or space, but is instantly and always with *every* believer. He could not come, however, until Jesus had ascended. Jesus Himself told His disciples, "Nevertheless I tell you the truth. It is to your advantage that I go away; for if I do not go away, the Helper will not come to you; but if I depart, I will send Him to you." [12] The Greek word for "Helper" is *parakletos*, which also means an advocate, a comforter, or an intercessor. It refers to someone who is called alongside to help another. This is a perfect description of what the Holy Spirit does in our lives.

The Holy Spirit came at Pentecost and has been here ever since, dwelling in the hearts of believers. However, I am convinced that today, two thousand years later, the Lord is blessing His people with a fresh visitation of holy wind and fire. We are in the beginning of a new millennium, and I believe that God is telling His Church that it is our hour to shine. In this end-times move of the Spirit, we are going to shine in the world for the glory of God as no other generation before us has done since the first century. The prophet Isaiah wrote, "Arise, shine; for your light has come! And the glory of the Lord is risen upon you."[13] In our day, the flame of the Holy Spirit will burn brighter in us than ever before, so that we truly will be the "light of the world" shining in the midst of the darkness.

This is no time for the Church to be halfhearted or noncommittal concerning the things of the Spirit. We have nothing to be ashamed of, nothing to apologize for. We should not be embarrassed or shy about the Holy Spirit. Instead, we should welcome Him and willingly allow Him to complete in us the work He was sent to do: equip the Church to reach the world with the gospel, and prepare the Church as a pure and spotless Bride, ready for the coming of Christ, her Bridegroom.

The Transformation of Pitcairn Island

On JANUARY 15, 1790, a small British ship dropped anchor off shore of a tiny deserted island in the South Pacific. Located roughly halfway between New Zealand and Chile, Pitcairn Island is one of the most isolated places on earth. The ship was the HMS *Bounty*, and those aboard had chosen Pitcairn Island specifically because of its remoteness.

Of the 28 people aboard, 9 were British seamen; the others were natives of Tahiti—12 women, 6 men, and 1 baby. The 9 seamen, including Master's Mate Fletcher Christian, were part of the band of mutineers who had seized the ship the previous April and cast adrift in a longboat its commander, William Bligh, and 18 others who had remained loyal to him.

After seizing the *Bounty*, Christian and the other mutineers sailed back to Tahiti, which they had left only a few weeks before. Several of the mutineers chose to stay on Tahiti. The others picked up their Polynesian passengers and sailed off to find a quiet, unknown place where they would never be found. Pitcairn Island seemed to be the perfect choice. A virtual paradise, with abundant food and water, the island was located far from any regular shipping routes.

Things did not go well, however. Before long, one of the sailors began distilling alcohol, and drunkenness quickly became a problem. Only three years after arriving on the island, the Tahitian men, angered by the ill treatment they and the women had received at the hands of the Europeans, rose up and killed Christian and several of the other mutineers. All six of the Tahitian men subsequently died violent deaths at one time or another. Soon, only four Europeans remained. One of them got drunk and committed suicide. Another, who had a dangerously violent temper, was killed by the other two. Then one of the two remaining mutineers died of asthma. By the year 1800, John Adams was the only surviving European on the island, and he was in charge of a small company of women and children. Most of the children had been fathered by the mutineers. Paradise had not lasted long.

Now jump ahead a few years. In 1808 the USS *Topaz*, an American whaling ship, stopped at Pitcairn Island, the first vessel of any kind to appear since the *Bounty* herself, 18 years earlier. Coming ashore, the crew of the *Topaz* found a flourishing and prosperous Christian community. There were no jails, no debauchery, no whiskey, no crime, no laziness.

41

The Hidden Power of the Believer's Touch

Worship, Bible reading, and prayer were a regular routine of Pitcairn life. Peace, harmony, and a Christ-like spirit pervaded the island. What had happened?

Several years earlier, John Adams, who had always been an irreligious man, had found the ship's Bible from the *Bounty*. Reading it, he had found Christ, received the Holy Spirit, and in a short time the entire island was converted. With no outside influences to hinder it, Pitcairn society flourished according to Christian principles and biblical teaching. Because one worldly, almost illiterate sailor found the Word of God, the Holy Spirit came and transformed the entire island.

The Fruit of Fellowship

THE STORY OF PITCAIRN ISLAND ILLUSTRATES on a small scale what the Holy Spirit can and wants to do on a global scale. He has the power to transform neighborhoods, communities, and even entire nations. His strategy is to touch people individually, one at a time, and transform them from the inside out. When we receive the Holy Spirit, He changes our hearts and begins working to mold us into the likeness of Christ. The primary work of the Holy Spirit is to make us like Jesus. He gives spiritual gifts *to* us so that we can do the work of Christ, and produces spiritual fruit *in* us so that we can look and act like Christ. Because He is the Spirit of Christ, He reproduces the life of Christ in us.

One of the ways the Holy Spirit makes us like Jesus is by planting in us a desire to be around other Christians. Christ the Son enjoys unbroken fellowship with God the Father and with the Holy Spirit. Fellowship is the environment of Heaven. Our Lord longs for fellowship with us, too. It is only natural, then, that the Holy Spirit would fill us with a desire for that same fellowship. He wants to create among believers on earth the same kind of fellowship found in Heaven. John described it this way:

> *That which we have seen and heard we declare to you, that you also may have fellowship with us; and truly our fellowship is with the Father and with His Son Jesus Christ....But if we walk in the light as He is in the light, we have fellowship with one*

another, and the blood of Jesus Christ His Son cleanses us from all sin.[14]

When we become believers, we want to be around other believers. We want to worship with other worshipers. When we are baptized in the Holy Spirit, we want to be around other Spirit-baptized people. We want to be a part of a group of people who are serving and obeying the Lord, reaching out to the world, and blessing humanity wherever they are. A desire in our hearts for fellowship with other believers is a sign that the Spirit is working in us.

Another sign of the Spirit's work in us is a growing desire for fellowship with Christ. It is a natural law that we all tend to become like the people we spend our time with. The only way to become like Jesus is to spend time with Him. It is the Holy Spirit who plants that desire in our heart. Once we receive Christ as our Savior, we want to be with Him. As we grow in faith, and learn to walk in the Spirit, we will want to spend more and more time with Him. The more time we spend with Jesus, the more we will love Him, and the more we love Him, the more our desire will grow for fellowship with Him.

What the Lord desires is that we walk so close to Him, and are so filled with His anointing, that He can live the fullness of His life *through* us! This means that as we learn to walk in the Spirit's anointing, everything Jesus *was* and *did* when He was on the earth can flow through us. He wants us to be conduits through whom His love, grace, mercy, and power pour out like a flood—"rivers of living water"[15] to inundate a lost and hurting world.

Deep Things of God Revealed

ONE OF THE PRIMARY MINISTRIES of the Holy Spirit in our lives is to reveal the deep things of God, truths about God which cannot be understood or known by natural means. God's saving grace, tender mercy, compassionate love; God's heart and mind, His thoughts which are not as our thoughts, and His ways which are not as our ways; these are some of the "deep things of God" that the Spirit reveals. Although they are beyond the comprehension of those who do not know the Lord, these things are the *birthright* of all of God's children. He loves us and wants us to know Him fully and to understand who we are in Him.

The apostle Paul explained it to the Corinthian believers this way:

But as it is written: "Eye has not seen, nor ear heard, nor have entered into the heart of man the things which God has prepared for those who love Him." But God has revealed them to us through His Spirit. For the Spirit searches all things, yes, the deep things of God. For what man knows the things of a man except the spirit of the man which is in him? Even so no one knows the things of God except the Spirit of God. Now we have received, not the spirit of the world, but the Spirit who is from God, that we might know the things that have been freely given to us by God. These things we also speak, not in words which man's wisdom teaches but which the Holy Spirit teaches, comparing spiritual things with spiritual. But the natural man does not receive the things of the Spirit of God, for they are foolishness to him; nor can he know them, because they are spiritually discerned. But he who is spiritual judges all things, yet he himself is rightly judged by no one. For "who has known the mind of the Lord that he may instruct Him?" But we have the mind of Christ.[16]

God has prepared for us things that are beyond our wildest imagination. There is no way we can know or understand them on our own. The Holy Spirit, however, "searches...the deep things of God," and He alone knows them. When we receive the Holy Spirit, we gain access to the deep things of God, because the Spirit reveals them to us. This is according to God's will, because He wants us to be aware of everything He has freely given us.

This passage reveals three absolutely incredible things the Spirit does for us. First, He *reveals* the deep things of God to us. Second, He *teaches* us what they are and enables us to understand them. But He doesn't stop there. Finally, and best of all, the Spirit gives us the *mind of Christ*!

So, what does it mean to have the mind of Christ? It means that we can learn to think the way He thinks, to fill our minds with thoughts of

God, of His love and compassion, and of His holiness and purity. It means to dwell on loving God and living in absolute surrender to His will. Having the mind of Christ means keeping our thoughts on the highest plane. In the words of Paul, "whatever things are true, whatever things are noble, whatever things are just, whatever things are pure, whatever things are lovely, whatever things are of good report, if there is any virtue and if there is anything praiseworthy—meditate on these things."[17]

Most of all, however, having the mind of Christ means giving our lives in self-sacrificing service as servants of God. Once again, Paul states it so well.

> *Let this mind be in you which was also in Christ Jesus, who, being in the form of God, did not consider it robbery to be equal with God, but made Himself of no reputation, taking the form of a bondservant, and coming in the likeness of men. And being found in appearance as a man, He humbled Himself and became obedient to the point of death, even the death of the cross.*[18]

No matter what our ministry or service, whether preaching, healing, prophesying, or whatever, we cannot do it under the anointing of the Spirit until and unless we are willing to lay down our lives in complete surrender to the will of Christ. One of the reasons so many Christians feel frustrated with their spiritual lives is because they have not learned to walk in the Spirit. Whether it is from lack of faith or just simple disobedience, many believers struggle daily with no sense of spiritual maturity, victory, or even God's presence in their lives. Unknowingly, many have allowed satan to rob them of their inheritance, to steal their understanding of their heritage as children of God and heirs to the Kingdom of Heaven.

The Holy Spirit Is Our Teacher

NOT ONLY DOES THE HOLY SPIRIT REVEAL the things of God to us and give us the mind of Christ, He also teaches us what all these things mean so that we can understand who we are and how we should live as kids of the King. Children born to royal families receive special education and training so they will know how to conduct themselves in a manner appropriate to their station. It is the same way with the Spirit. He guides us and instructs us so that our lives will reflect the nature and character of our Father.

The Spirit's teaching is at a level and dimension unknown and incomprehensible to the world. Only the Spirit can reveal the things of the Spirit. We cannot discover them on our own. As Paul explained, "These things we also speak, not in words which man's wisdom teaches but which the Holy Spirit teaches, comparing spiritual things with spiritual. But the natural man does not receive the things of the Spirit of God, for they are foolishness to him; nor can he know them, because they are spiritually discerned."[19]

As the Spirit works in our hearts, He teaches us the qualities of life in the heavenly Kingdom. "But the fruit of the Spirit is love, joy, peace, longsuffering, kindness, goodness, faithfulness, gentleness, self-control. Against such there is no law."[20] The world has its own versions of these qualities, but they are only dim and inferior copies because they lack the spiritual spark and vigor of the originals. As the Spirit produces His fruit in us, we come to understand what they *really* mean. People outside God's Kingdom need to know what *true* love is, and what *true* joy and peace are like. The only way they *can* know is to see them on display in us.

The Holy Spirit is Heaven's emissary, through whom all the things of God come to us.

- He gives us wisdom and spiritual knowledge: "that the God of our Lord Jesus Christ, the Father of glory, may give to you the spirit of wisdom and revelation in the knowledge of Him."[21]

- He teaches us about Jesus and helps us know Him better: "But when the Helper comes, whom I shall send to you from the Father, the Spirit of truth who proceeds from the Father, He will testify of Me. And you also will bear witness, because you have been with Me from the beginning."[22]

- He teaches us all things and reminds us of Jesus' words: "But the Helper, the Holy Spirit, whom the Father will send in My name, He will teach you all things, and bring to your remembrance all things that I said to you."[23]

- He guides us into all the truth: "However, when He, the Spirit of truth, has come, He will guide you into all truth; for He will not speak on His own authority, but whatever He hears He will speak; and He will tell you things to come."[24]

- He gives us assurance that we belong to Christ: "The Spirit Himself bears witness with our spirit that we are children of God, and if children, then heirs—heirs of God and joint heirs with Christ."[25]

The Holy Spirit teaches us that we are children of royalty, and helps us learn how to walk, talk, and behave accordingly. We are not orphans or beggars. We are sons and daughters of the King of kings. The God of the galaxies is our Father.

The Power of Knowledge

A N OLD ADAGE SAYS, "Knowledge is power." This is certainly true in the spiritual realm. Once we know who we are in Christ, that knowledge awakens in us an awareness of the spiritual authority we have as God's children. That authority enables us, among other things, to speak life and health into our lives and circumstances, as well as those of others. When we recognize the authority we have, we can do battle with the devil in the power of the Spirit and be confident of victory.

When my wife, Bonnie, was pregnant with Anna, our second child, at one point it appeared as though our baby had died in the womb. There was no apparent movement, and the doctors could detect no heartbeat. In fact, they could detect nothing at all—no signs of life. You can imagine how we felt. The devil was bombarding our minds and our spirits with the message, "Your baby is dead." On the other hand, the Holy Spirit had revealed to us that Jesus came to give us abundant life.[26] So right away we were engaged in a battle on the spiritual level.

I said, "Devil, you are a liar and the father of lies. You've always been a liar, and you're lying right now. Jesus came to give our babies life. We speak life into this womb." I remember putting my hands on Bonnie's stomach and saying, "There's life. That baby is alive. I don't care what they are saying. I don't care whether you don't feel a thing. That baby is going to live and is going to be healthy." (Then the Lord said, "And she's going to be good-looking too!")

Seriously, though, when Anna was born, she had every finger and every toe. Everything was in place, right where it was supposed to be. She had a strong heartbeat and a healthy cry! In short, Anna was completely whole. Today, she is a healthy, happy, and quite beautiful young lady. But we had to battle against the lying spirit of the devil. We probably would have lost that battle except that the Holy Spirit had revealed to us the rights, benefits, and authority that were ours as children of God. By the authority of Jesus' name and in the power of the Spirit we were able to go against the devil, speak life into Bonnie's womb, and prevail.

Knowledge really *is* power. We cannot hope to prevail in our daily battles with the devil if we don't *know* that as children of God we have authority over him in the name of Jesus. We won't see many miracles of healing or walk in the healing anointing if we don't know and believe that He who is in us is greater than he who is in the world.[27] The Holy Spirit makes these things known to us. This revelation is not only for us, however, but for our children, our neighbors, and for any who are broken-hearted, or who are slaves to sin or sickness. We can do battles on their behalf and bring them into their inheritance in God.

The Holy Spirit came, in part, to fulfill Christ's promise that we would do the same works He did, and greater works, because He was going back to His Father.[28] I believe that the "works" and the "greater works" include healing. The purpose of Pentecost was to give to us the Person of the Holy Spirit, who imparts to us the power and authority to do the works of Jesus. Part of that authority is the authority to heal, to touch the sick around us. If we want to learn to walk in the healing anointing, we need to understand the *authority* we have for healing.

Endnotes

1. Ps. 1:3.
2. Rev. 22:1-2.
3. Jn. 7:37b-38.
4. Jn. 7:39.
5. Lk. 24:49.
6. Acts 1:4-5,8.
7. Is. 44:3-4.
8. Ezek. 36:27-28.
9. Joel 2:28-29.
10. Acts 2:1-4.
11. See Mt. 26:69-70.
12. Jn. 16:7.
13. Is. 60:1.
14. 1 Jn. 1:3,7.
15. Jn. 7:38b.
16. 1 Cor. 2:9-16.
17. Phil. 4:8.
18. Phil. 2:5-8.
19. 1 Cor. 2:13-14.
20. Gal. 5:22-23.
21. Eph. 1:17.
22. Jn. 15:26-27.

23. Jn. 14:26.
24. Jn. 16:13.
25. Rom. 8:16-17a.
26. See Jn. 10:10.
27. See 1 Jn. 4:4.
28. See Jn. 14:12.

Chapter Four

The Authority to Heal

WHENEVER WE SURRENDER TO THE FLOW of the river of God, the Spirit of God will take us where He wants us to go. Sometimes He takes us through the place of blessings, where we find refreshing and renewal, and receive fresh anointing and impartation of the Lord's power and presence. At other times He leads us to other people who need a touch from God: the lost, the sick, the hurting, the hungry, the poor, the down-and-out, and the destitute. The first destination is easy and fun; the second one is not. What Christian doesn't like to soak in the cool pools of God's blessing? It's a lot harder to leave those pools and venture into the parched, arid ground of the spiritually starved. Many believers don't even try. Instead, they are content to stay "in the river, " gorging themselves on the *good* things of God. In the process, they miss out on the *better* things of God: the joy of being an obedient servant and witnessing the transformation of spiritually hungry people by the power of God. I can speak from personal experience that there is nothing better than being a willing vessel whom God uses to help bring salvation and healing to others.

During our adventure on the river, we will encounter triumph and joy, as well as sorrow and heartbreak along the way. As long as we remember that the Lord is the captain of our expedition, and that He knows what He is doing and where He is going, if we follow along in faith and obedience, He will lead us into the fullness of His purpose. Only through faith and obedience can any of us know the deep things of God, or learn to recognize and walk in the authority He has given us. It requires patience and discipline, and a daily walking in the Spirit, waiting for the Lord's timing.

The Story of Three Sons

IN 1984 I WAS DOING HEALING MINISTRY in the African nation of Zambia. One night around midnight a local missionary knocked on my door and asked me to accompany him to a small village in the bush. A woman in the village had heard about our ministry and had asked if I would come and pray for her son, who was dying.

When we arrived in the village and entered the woman's hut, we found her holding the body of her son, who had died about two hours earlier. The boy was a victim of cerebral malaria, the kind of malaria that cooks the brain. He was only five years old, one of a set of twins. In that part of Africa, many people did not understand the occurrence of twins; they considered it a curse. For this reason, the woman's husband had divorced her and sent her back to her home village. She was a single mother trying to care for her children, and now one of them had died.

I held the child in my arms for several hours, praying and crying out to the Lord to do something. Nothing happened. Finally, I gave the boy back to his mother. She wept and said, "He will no longer come to me, but I will go to him." This woman had been a Christian for only about six months. I knew during that time she had not had the opportunity to learn much Scripture, yet she had just echoed the words of David in Second Samuel 12:23 when he was mourning the death of his infant son born to Bathsheba.

I felt so bad for this grieving mother. Confused, I stepped out of the hut. Inside I was crying for her, and crying out to the Lord. Just then the Lord's voice blew like a gentle breeze in my spirit and said, "I will comfort her." Then He said to me, "Because you have been faithful, I will let you see great things." At the time I did not understand the fullness or depth of that promise. I simply had to trust the Lord to bring it to pass in His time.

The following January I received a letter from some believers in Zaire, a nation to the northwest of Zambia, asking me to hold a crusade in their country. The letter was on very poor quality paper and was hard to read, but said, "The Lord has told us that if you come, the history of our nation will change." Judging from the quality of the letter, I thought it would be a miracle if they were able to get even six hundred people together for a meeting. Nevertheless, I prayed about it and was surprised when the Lord said, "Go." So I accepted the invitation.

A few weeks later, Bonnie and I learned that she was pregnant with our fourth child, Aaron. About three months into the pregnancy Bonnie developed complications that confined her to bed for three months. Despite our prayers, her condition worsened. She began to suffer severe bleeding, and at one point part of the placenta came out. The doctor feared that Bonnie might die, so he put her in the hospital. A week later, Aaron was born three months premature.

At birth Aaron weighed only one pound, three ounces and, to be honest, he looked like a tiny, squashed rat. He was about the size of the palm of my hand. From the very first, life was a struggle for him. His lungs had not formed. Every breath he took was a great effort; it looked as though he could die at any moment. Parts of his stomach and intestines had died, and the doctor had to go in and cut away the dead parts. He had a brain hemorrhage. We were told that Aaron would die in a matter of hours, or almost certainly within a few days. Even if he did survive, he would probably be a vegetable.

My wife was not out of danger yet, my infant son was barely clinging to life, and I was committed to go to Africa. I had made a commitment to minister there with Derek Prince, and he was depending on me to bear part of the weight of the ministry. I couldn't let him down. Besides, Bonnie and I both had committed our lives long ago to follow the Lord wherever He led us. It was not easy for me to leave Bonnie and Aaron during such a time, but I knew I had to go. Bonnie took my hand

and said, "Honey, we have to obey the heavenly vision. We have been called. Your place is in Africa. You have to go."

As I prepared to leave, I hurt inside because, as far as I knew, Bonnie would have to bury Aaron alone. I went into the special little room where Aaron was under constant nurse's care. I wanted to spend a final few minutes with him. As I anointed my son with oil, I said to him, "Aaron, it looks like I will not see you again, but if I don't see you here, I'll see you in Heaven. I want you to know that I love you, but I'm putting you in the hands of someone who loves you even more. I'm putting you in the hands of Jesus." Then I left immediately for the airport, flew to Africa, and met Derek to begin our ministry together in Zambia.

Two and a half weeks later, Derek and I had split up, he to hold a crusade in Zimbabwe, while I fulfilled my commitment in Zaire. I must admit, I really wasn't expecting anything big to happen. Aside from the original letter, there had been very little communication about the meetings. So, I was relieved when the organizers met me at the airport.

We conducted two meetings a day during the weeklong crusade: a training session for leaders in the morning, and a larger, open evangelistic meeting in the evening. On the very first night, one hundred thousand people came! By the end of the week, nearly 360,000 people were attending. The Zairian army, which was present to handle crowd control, verified this figure.

The presence and power of God were evident from the beginning. One woman, eaten up with cancer, was instantly and completely healed. Several people, crippled from birth, received healing and, witnessed by thousands, walked and ran for the first time in their lives. On one night alone, 25,000 came to Christ!

During the Wednesday morning leaders' session, I was speaking to the crowd of over thirty thousand, when I sensed a change in the atmosphere. It was around noon. I stopped speaking and stepped back from the microphone. I was suddenly aware of the presence of the glory of the Lord. It swept over me in the same gentle breeze as a year earlier outside the hut of the woman whose son had died. The crowd was before me, but

I could not hear them. All I heard was the voice of the Lord. In the midst of my pain and hurt over Bonnie and Aaron, who was struggling for life halfway around the world, the Lord said to me, "There is a man here whose son died this morning. Call him up. This day I am going to resurrect his son!"

What else could I do but obey? I said, "Where is the man whose son died this morning? Come forward, and the Lord will do something wonderful. This day He will resurrect your son." In Africa, if you speak a word like this before thirty thousand people, something had better happen, or you had better not come back! A man rushed forward from the crowd. We learned that his six-year-old son, Katshinyi, had died of cerebral malaria at four o'clock that very morning.

This grieving father had been sitting in the hospital with the body of his son when he heard the Lord say, "My servant is in this city; go to him." So the father left Katshinyi's body in the care of the boy's uncle, who was an unbeliever, and hurried to our meeting site. It was noon when I called the father forward; his son had been dead for *eight hours*. At the very same moment that I laid hands on his father, Katshinyi sneezed twice, woke up as if he had been asleep, and said, "Where is my daddy?" Then he said, "I'm hungry." Just as He had promised, God had miraculously raised Katshinyi from the dead!

That very day the unbelieving uncle came to Christ. Thousands of others were saved as well. Nearly a hundred churches were birthed through this miracle and the others that occurred that week.[1] At the same time, as I learned later, the Lord reached down and completely restored Aaron. He was totally healed. Today, he is a robust and healthy young man.

Obedience Releases Miracle Power

IF THERE IS ONE THING that the story of the three sons demonstrates, it is that healing and other miracles come from God *alone*. No human being possesses such power or authority; they are the domain and prerogative of God only. Although I was involved in the circumstances of all three sons, I did not determine their outcomes. In the first case, I prayed, but to no avail. God allowed the child to go. With Aaron, I also prayed, but in the end all I could do was say goodbye to him, expecting never to see him alive again. God, in His infinite love and mercy, chose to heal and restore Aaron completely. I had nothing to do with it. Where Katshinyi was concerned, I simply obeyed the Word of the Lord. As I placed my hands on Katshinyi's father, God raised Katshinyi from the dead, miles away.

A second truth that we can draw from this story is that obedience to the Lord is critical to the release of His miracle power in and through our lives. Our God is a miracle-working God, but He always seeks willing servants, open and available vessels through whom He can work. Through His Spirit, God has given us His authority. Many believers never appropriate that authority due either to ignorance or unbelief. Both are hindrances to walking in the anointing. We have to believe before we can receive.

Believing Is Seeing

WE'VE ALL HEARD THE OLD SAYING, "Seeing is believing." That's not always true, especially in the spiritual realm. In the Kingdom of God, it would be more accurate to say, "Believing is seeing." Spiritual eyes of faith do not require visual proof (such as miracles) in order to believe. Sometimes, however, visual proof helps strengthen and confirm the faith of those who are already inclined to believe.

Jesus consistently rewarded genuine faith, no matter how small. When the father of a boy who was possessed with a mute spirit cried desperately, "Lord, I believe; help my unbelief!"[2] Jesus cast out the spirit and restored the boy to wholeness. When a woman who had suffered from severe hemorrhaging for twelve years simply touched the hem of Jesus' robe and was instantly healed, He turned to her and said, "Be of good cheer, daughter; your faith has made you well."[3] Jesus never turned away or refused a cry for help that was offered in faith.

On the other hand, Jesus consistently refused to perform miracles on demand. This was one of the temptations of satan that He overcame in the wilderness. Miracles were an accompaniment to faith; Jesus never performed them for their own sake. In fact, He had harsh words for those who demanded such signs. "A wicked and adulterous generation seeks after a sign, and no sign shall be given to it except the sign of the prophet Jonah."[4]

Such a demand came from people like the scribes and Pharisees, whose hearts were hardened in unbelief. They neither believed in Jesus nor had any intention of doing so. Jesus, therefore, refused to accommodate them.

Believing *is* seeing. Faith releases in us the capacity to see truth in the spiritual realm that would otherwise be hidden. Faith reveals Jesus to us. It opens up to us the very heart of God. These are things that are unknown and incomprehensible to unbelievers. Spiritual truth is spiritually discerned; faith is required. Without faith, even people who witness a miracle will misunderstand it. There is no biblical evidence of any unbeliever ever being convinced or converted by the witness of a miracle *alone*. That is why the Pharisees could watch Jesus perform a miracle and completely miss the point. One Sabbath, when Jesus healed a man in the synagogue who had a withered hand, all the Pharisees could see was that Jesus had broken the law by healing (working) on the Sabbath.[5] The truth that the Kingdom of Heaven was near and that the Messiah was in their very midst was utterly beyond them.

God reserves the greatest blessings for those who believe without requiring proof first. Many people have called the apostle Thomas, "Doubting Thomas," because he refused to believe the testimonies of the other disciples that Jesus had risen from the dead. He said, "Unless I see in His hands the print of the nails, and put my finger into the print of the nails, and put my hand into His side, I will not believe."[6] A week later, Jesus appeared to Thomas and invited him to do just that. Upon seeing Jesus, Thomas declared his faith in his risen Lord. Jesus replied, "Thomas, because you have seen Me, you have believed. Blessed are those who have not seen and yet have believed."[7]

Believing *is* seeing. Faith opens the door to the anointing, the blessings, the wisdom, the power, and the miracles of God.

The Problem With Faith

THOMAS WAS NOT THE ONLY DISCIPLE who had some problems with his faith. There were others who struggled as well. "Then the eleven disciples went away into Galilee, to the mountain which Jesus had appointed for them. When they saw Him, they worshiped Him; but some doubted."[8] These were the men who had lived with Jesus, walked with Him, learned from Him, and witnessed numerous signs and miracles from His hand. They had even experienced His power for themselves when Jesus commissioned them to preach and gave them authority to cast out demons and to heal the sick.[9] They had witnessed the crucifixion. After the resurrection, Jesus had appeared to them and shown them the nail prints in His hands. They had *seen* Him alive with their own eyes. Yet, despite all of this evidence, some still doubted.

Faith is not always easy; we have to guard it carefully every day. In our modern age, and especially in our Western culture here in America, we are brainwashed daily with the spirits of doubt, unbelief, and humanism. These are extremely potent forces of evil, primary weapons in the arsenal of the powers of darkness that are all around us. We must learn to stand firm against them if we are determined to move in the revelation of Jesus Christ.

For Western Christians, belief in miracles, signs, and wonders is often the hardest aspect of the faith to affirm. If we accept the Bible as the Word of God, it is easy enough to accept the truth of the miracles recorded there. Moses, Elijah, and Elisha performed miracles. So did Jesus, Peter, Paul, and others. We have no problem with that. Where we run into trouble is when we start to rationalize away these truths for our own day. "Well, that was then; this is now." "We don't need signs and wonders today; we have the completed Word of God." "Miracles are not for today. They were only needed in the first century to help establish the Church." "Miracles may happen in Africa or India, but they don't happen in America." "Even if miracles *do* occur today, I will probably never see one." "I'm not a great saint like Peter or Paul; I shouldn't expect the Lord to use me the way He used them." If we are not careful, negative thoughts and assumptions such as these will eat away at our spirits until we are consumed with doubt and unbelief.

Consider this: Whenever we affirm our faith in the Lord Jesus, we affirm our faith in miracles. Jesus Himself is a miracle. His Incarnation is a miracle. His death for our sins is a miracle. His resurrection is a miracle. The miracle of Jesus Christ is not confined to the first century. Jesus is *still* the Word who became flesh; He is *still* the Lamb of God who takes away the sin of the world; He is *still* the risen King who is alive from the dead!

Whenever we affirm that Jesus saves sinners, we affirm our faith in miracles, because salvation itself is a miracle. Salvation is not a natural process with its source in man, but a supernatural process with its source in God. "But as many as received Him, to them He gave the right to become children of God, to those who believe in His name: who were born, not of blood, nor of the will of the flesh, nor of the will of man, but of God."[10]

If *these* miracles continue today, why not the *others*? God hasn't changed. "Jesus Christ is the same yesterday, today, and forever."[11] Every miracle I've seen in Africa, I've seen in America, because God loves Americans just as much as He loves Africans. Miracles and healing *are* for us today, but we must exercise faith in order to release them in our lives or those of others.

Gary's Story[12]

I WANT TO TELL YOU A STORY about the healing of a man that I'll call Gary. His testimony is an excellent illustration not only of the Lord's power to heal today, but also of the importance of faith as part of the process.

Gary is a young man who was severely injured in a traffic accident. One day on the highway, a pickup truck pulled out in front of him. In the ensuing collision, Gary's face hit the steering wheel at 55 miles an hour. At the same time, the force of the impact caused his cerebrum, the upper portion of his brain, to shear partially away from the lower sections of his brain, the cerebellum and the medulla oblongata. Extensive plastic surgery was required to reconstruct Gary's face. Repairing the damage to his brain was another matter.

The cerebellum controls motor functions and coordination. Because of the partial separation of Gary's cerebrum from his cerebellum, he became subject to frequent, unpredictable, and severe episodes similar to epileptic seizures. He suffered severe headaches, blackouts, and loss of motor coordination. His face would swell at the places that were injured in the accident. His metabolic rate would drop and so would his body temperature. At first, his doctors told him it would wear off in time. It didn't. His condition finally reached the point where he was in danger of losing his job.

Gary believed in healing, and repeatedly sought anointing and prayer. Time after time he went forward for prayer, but nothing happened. After awhile, Gary's doctor, other people who had suffered similar injuries, and even his church began encouraging him to "accept" his condition. Gary refused to receive that. He still sought healing, but it still eluded him.

One night, Gary attended a healing service that I was holding. So many people had come forward for prayer that there was no more room down front. I said, "I'm sorry, there's no more room, but all of you who have head problems, stand in the aisles and receive your healing." Gary was so jaded by this time after two years of fruitless prayer, that at first he hesitated. His wife encouraged him to stand up, and he did so, but only as a "catcher" for the young woman in front of him, who suffered from migraines. As I prayed, Gary found himself interceding for her, and then she began praying for him.

At first, it seemed as though nothing had happened—until Gary moved back to his seat. Suddenly, he began to feel God working inside his head, touching and healing the sheared places in his brain. After that night, Gary was completely healed, and suffered no further attacks.

As Gary shared in a testimony a year later, the key to his healing lay in something that happened just a few days before he came to my meeting. God revealed to Gary that although he had diligently and persistently sought healing, he was not in the *place* of healing. Hebrews 11:6 says, "But without faith it is impossible to please Him, for he who comes to God must believe that He is, and that He is a rewarder of those who diligently seek Him." Gary was diligently seeking, but he had unconsciously developed an attitude that said, "God, you're supposed to heal. If you don't heal me, then you are not God in my life." In a very real sense he had denied the truth that God *is*. He had bound God's hands by saying, "You cannot be God unless you heal me."

When the Lord revealed this to Gary one night in a motel room at 2:00 a.m., Gary repented and prayed, "God, I make you God even if I am never healed." Once his faith was in the right place and his priorities in order, Gary was in the *place* of healing. Just a couple of days later, after more than two years of seeking, Gary received his healing.

All Authority Belongs to Jesus

THE AUTHORITY WE HAVE AS CHRISTIANS is a *delegated* and *imparted* authority; it does not originate with us. Gary was healed after he recognized and acknowledged God's absolute authority and lordship over his life. It is important that we do the same. Jesus imparted this truth to His disciples in some of His last words before His ascension.

> *And Jesus came and spoke to them, saying, "All authority has been given to Me in heaven and on earth. Go therefore and make disciples of all the nations, baptizing them in the name of the Father and of the Son and of the Holy Spirit, teaching them to observe all things that I have commanded you; and lo, I am with you always, even to the end of the age."[13]*

Jesus clearly stated that *all* authority has been given to Him. All means *all*! There is no authority that exists outside of the realm of the Lord Jesus Christ. Even in this world of ours, as evil, corrupt, and debased as it is, no authority exists except that of Christ. The devil has power, but he has no *authority*. Although he still holds millions of people in spiritual bondage and darkness, satan is living on borrowed time, clinging desperately to his steadily eroding power base. The Holy One invaded his domain two thousand years ago, and the devil has been losing ground ever since. It may not seem that way, considering the moral and spiritual condition of our world. However, the increasing darkness and hellishness of our world are signs of satan's increasing desperation. He knows he has lost and that his time is short, because the One who possesses *all* authority is on the scene.

One day the whole world will recognize and acknowledge Jesus' absolute authority. He is the One whom God has "highly exalted," and given the "name which is above every name," before whom *every* knee will bow and *every* tongue confess His lordship.[14]

Christ, to whom all authority has been given, has commanded us to "go therefore and make disciples of all the nations." He sends us both *in* and *with* His authority. "As the Father has sent Me, I also send you."[15] As we go, we have His authority to back us up. His promise, "Lo, I am with you always, even to the end of the age" is further proof that His authority stands behind us.

When the United States ambassador to another nation speaks in his official capacity, he does not speak in his own authority, but in the authority of the President. Behind his words stand the full authority and power of the United States government. In the same way, when we speak and act in Jesus' name, His full authority and power stand behind us. Jesus said, "And these signs will follow those who believe: In My name they will cast out demons; they will speak with new tongues; they will take up serpents; and if they drink anything deadly, it will by no means hurt them; they will lay hands on the sick, and they will recover."[16] "In My name" means the same thing as "with My authority." With His authority Jesus cast out demons, raised the dead, and healed the sick. With His authority, we will do the same.

It Comes Down to Us

THERE IS A PROGRESSION OF AUTHORITY that begins with the God the Father, passes on to Christ the Son, then to His disciples, and finally, to us. Jesus said, "All authority has been given to Me." He received it from His Father. Jesus' authority manifested itself in power through the anointing of the Holy Spirit. Jesus never healed or did any other sign or work except under the Spirit's anointing.

When the time came, Jesus delegated His authority to His disciples. "And when He had called His twelve disciples to Him, He gave them power over unclean spirits, to cast them out, and to heal all kinds of sickness and all kinds of disease.... 'Heal the sick, cleanse the lepers, raise the dead, cast out demons. Freely you have received, freely give.'"[17] The Greek word for "power" in this passage is *exousia*, which means power in the sense of delegated authority or jurisdiction.[18] The disciples went out in the authority of Jesus to preach, teach, and do the works that He did.

Later, Jesus expanded His delegation of authority beyond the 12 apostles.

> *After these things the Lord appointed seventy others also, and sent them two by two before His face into every city and place where He Himself was about to go.... "And heal the sick there, and say to them, 'The kingdom of God has come near to you....'" Then the seventy returned with joy, saying, "Lord, even the demons are subject to us in Your name."*[19]

Authority flowed from the Father, to Jesus, to the 12, and then to the 70. Finally, in His last and greatest commands, Jesus passed His authority to all believers of every generation: "Go therefore and make disciples of all the nations."[20] "Go into all the world and preach the gospel to every creature....And these signs will follow those who believe."[21]

It's high time for the Church to stop apologizing for the gospel and to take hold of our God-given authority to do the works of Jesus. As we seek to act on the Word of God for healing, and to flow with the healing presence of God, we must recognize the authority in which Jesus flowed, and understand how He passed that authority on to His disciples, and to us. We must also understand the importance of receiving, keeping, and walking in the anointing of the Spirit. Then we will see the love, grace, mercy, and healing power of God manifested in our own lives and circumstances, as well as in the lives and circumstances of all those to whom the Lord leads us to minister.

Endnotes

1. A fuller and more detailed account of this miracle is found in my book *Only Love Can Make a Miracle*. A copy of Katshinyi's death certificate is included. Mahesh Chavda with John Blattner, *Only Love Can Make a Miracle* (Ann Arbor, MI: Vine Books/Servant Publications, 1990).

2. Mk. 9:24b.

3. Mt. 9:22b.

4. Mt. 16:4a.

5. See Mk. 3:1-6.

6. Jn. 20:25b.

7. Jn. 20:29.

8. Mt. 28:16-17.

9. See Lk. 9:1-2.

10. Jn. 1:12-13.

11. Heb. 13:8.

12. "Gary" is not his real name. Although his testimony is true as presented, I have changed his name to protect his privacy.

13. Mt. 28:18-20.

14. See Phil. 2:9-11.

15. Jn. 20:21b.

16. Mk. 16:17-18.

17. Mt. 10:1,8.

18. Strong's Hebrew and Greek Dictionaries (Parson's Technology, Inc., Electronic Edition STEP Files, 1998). **exousia** (#G1849).

19. Lk. 10:1,9,17.

20. Mt. 28:19a.

21. Mk. 16:15b,17a.

Chapter Five

Receiving—and Keeping—the Anointing of the Lord

WE ALL NEED THE POWER OF GOD operating in our lives. In our own strength we are no match for the temptations of this world or for the evil one; we will lose every time. Our only hope is to lay hold of a power outside ourselves, a power greater than any human instrumentality. God has made such power—His power—available to us by His real and literal presence in us through His Spirit. The prophet Zechariah wrote, "'Not by might nor by power, but by My Spirit,' says the Lord of hosts."[1] Jesus promised His disciples, "You shall receive power when the Holy Spirit has come upon you."[2] Paul asked the Corinthians, "Do you not know that you are the temple of God and that the Spirit of God dwells in you?"[3]

If it is true that the Spirit of God dwells in us, then why do so many of us see so little evidence of His presence? One of the most common complaints among Western Christians is the lack of spiritual power in their lives. Many have little sense of the ongoing presence of the Lord. They feel that they are not growing spiritually, and only rarely do they experience spiritual victory. I have found even among "charismatics" a great disillusionment with their Christian lives. Many have eagerly received and embraced the anointing of the Spirit only to see that anointing lift and depart later. They wonder why they can't seem to "hold onto" the anointing.

Part of the problem, I believe, is that many Christians simply do not know or understand the Person of the Holy Spirit. To them He is a mysterious and somewhat "spooky" entity that they would rather not talk about. Another cause of spiritual disillusionment is a misunderstanding of the nature and purpose of the anointing. As long as we think of the anointing as something given primarily to make us feel good, we will never be able to "hold onto" it. The harder we try to hoard it for ourselves, the faster it will slip away. The only way to *keep* the anointing is to *give it away*.

A third reason for the lack of spiritual power among many believers is the influence of the world. The Lord gave me a word one time, and said, "My people have been brainwashed by humanism, by the educational system, by television, and by the thoughts of the ungodly. But I am going to raise up an army of blood-washed people." The negative, depressing, and ungodly philosophies and attitudes of the world have dulled our spiritual senses, causing us to lose sight of God's perspective. The Lord wants His people to be *blood-washed*, not brainwashed. He wants us to be blood-cleansed and power-anointed.

You probably remember the saying, "Beauty is only skin deep, but ugly goes clear to the bone!" Well, the Lord wants us to be so full of His Spirit that His anointing will not rest just on the surface, but soak us "clear to the bone." We should be like Holy Ghost sponges, so saturated with the anointing that wherever we go we will give off the sweet fragrance of the Spirit.

A Double Portion of the Anointing

THE LIFE OF THE OLD TESTAMENT PROPHET ELISHA serves as a great illustration of the power of the anointing. Let's begin, however, with his death.

> *Then Elisha died, and they buried him. And the raiding bands from Moab invaded the land in the spring of the year. So it was, as they were burying a man, that suddenly they spied a band of*

raiders; and they put the man in the tomb of Elisha; and when the man was let down and touched the bones of Elisha, he revived and stood on his feet.[4]

Elisha, the prophetic successor to Elijah, was filled "clear to the bone" with the anointing of the Spirit. The anointing so permeated Elisha that it remained on his bones even after his death. It was so powerful, in fact, that a dead man whose corpse touched Elisha's bones was brought back to life.

Years earlier, this same Elisha had boldly asked for a double portion of the anointing which was on Elijah, his teacher and mentor. It was not an idle request. By his persistence, Elisha demonstrated his willingness to pay any price for the Lord's anointing.

And it came to pass, when the Lord was about to take up Elijah into heaven by a whirlwind, that Elijah went with Elisha from Gilgal. Then Elijah said to Elisha, "Stay here, please, for the Lord has sent me on to Bethel." But Elisha said, "As the Lord lives, and as your soul lives, I will not leave you!" So they went down to Bethel.[5]

When tested, Elisha proved his mettle. Elisha refused to leave Elijah's side. Wherever Elijah went, Elisha went. At Bethel, the Lord told Elijah to go to Jericho, and from Jericho to the Jordan. In both instances, Elijah tried to persuade Elisha to stay behind. In both instances Elisha's response was the same as when He was asked to stay in Gilgal: "As the Lord lives, and as your soul lives, I will not leave you!"[6]

Finally, at the Jordan River, Elijah touched his mantle to the water, the waters separated, and he and Elisha crossed over on dry land. [7]

And so it was, when they had crossed over, that Elijah said to Elisha, "Ask! What may I do for you, before I am taken away from you?" Elisha said, "Please let a double portion of your spirit be upon me." So he said, "You have asked a hard thing. Nevertheless, if you see me when I am taken from you, it shall be so for you; but if not, it shall not be so." Then it happened, as they continued on and talked, that suddenly a chariot of fire appeared with horses of fire, and separated the two of them; and Elijah went up by a whirlwind into heaven.[8]

Elisha's persistence paid off. He had paid the price and his bold request was granted. He received double the anointing which had been on Elijah. Because of his willingness to surrender completely to the will of the Lord, Elisha received the complete anointing. From this point on, Elisha went forth and did greater miracles than Elijah had done. He healed bitter water and barren ground.[9] He multiplied the volume of oil in a small jar for a widow and her sons so they could earn money to live on.[10] Elisha prophesied the birth of a son to a barren Shunammite woman,[11] and later raised that same son from the dead.[12] He detoxified a poisonous stew and multiplied 20 loaves of barley bread and a little bit of grain to feed 100 men.[13] He was instrumental in healing the Syrian general Naaman of leprosy.[14] It was not because of any special qualities or powers of his own that Elisha did these things, but because the *powerful anointing of God* rested on him and filled him.

In the same way, the Lord wants to fill and permeate each of us so that He can perform great works through us and touch the lives of millions. It is not by any works of righteousness that we do or any special merit or standing that we have on our own, but by the Lord's anointing. It is not by our might or our power, but by His Spirit. A long time ago, the Lord gave me a prophetic word about the anointing. He said, "The people who surrender completely to Me are the ones who will flow in My complete anointing." Complete surrender leads to complete anointing. This is the kind of sold-out, blood-cleansed, and power-anointed, end-time army whom God wants to raise up in our generation.

An Anointed Bride, Fit for the King

GOD'S ANOINTED, END-TIME ARMY IS A MASSIVE ARMY, unlike any other army the world has ever seen. Made up of the people of God throughout the world, this army will conquer not by military might or human schemes, but by the power of the Holy Spirit. Our weapons will not be bullets, bombs, missiles, and fear, but love, grace, mercy, and self-sacrifice. In other words, as soldiers of the Lord, we will follow the strategy already laid out and executed by our Commander-in-Chief, Jesus Christ.

The Bible pictures the Church in another way as well. Not only are we the army of the Lord, we are also the Bride of Christ.

> *Then I, John, saw the holy city, New Jerusalem, coming down out of heaven from God, prepared as a bride adorned for her husband....Then one of the seven angels...came to me and talked with me, saying, "Come, I will show you the bride, the Lamb's wife." And he carried me away in the Spirit to a great and high mountain, and showed me the great city, the holy Jerusalem, descending out of heaven from God, having the glory of God.*[15]

I once received a vision from the Lord regarding the Church, in which He said, "This is My end-time Bride, My Church. She will be equally yoked with Me, and the anointing that is upon Me will be upon her." We're not talking about only a few privileged individuals here, but the entire corporate Body of Christ. *We* are His Bride, and His anointing is upon all of us—you, me, and everyone else who claims the name of Jesus.

The Holy Spirit is the one who prepares the Bride for her Bridegroom. He adorns her with gifts. He purifies her, cleanses her, and makes her beautiful, so that when the Bridegroom comes, He will find her ready and waiting, without spot or blemish.

We find a wonderful picture of this process in the Book of Esther. After Esther, a young Jewish maiden, was chosen for the harem of the Persian king, she had to go through months of preparation before she was ready to be presented to the king. One of the king's eunuchs, Hegai, who was in charge of the care and preparation of the young women in the harem, was particularly taken with Esther and showed her special favor.

For a full 12 months each woman was given beauty treatments, which included soaking in myrrh and fine perfumes, so that her skin would be beautiful and would exude a sweet fragrance for the king. Each one also received an allowance from the treasury. They were taught how to behave in the presence of the king, and how to present themselves to him in an appealing yet appropriate manner. Under Hegai's careful guidance, Esther outshone the others in beauty, poise, and grace. When finally she went in to the king, he was so delighted with her that he made Esther his wife and queen.

In this picture, Hegai the eunuch represents the Holy Spirit. Hegai's job was to prepare Esther to be the bride of the king. The Holy Spirit's job is to prepare the Bride of Christ to meet her Bridegroom, the King of kings. Like the fine myrrh and other perfumes of Esther's day, the Spirit's anointing makes the Bride a sweet fragrance to her King. After long preparation the Bride is ready. She eagerly awaits her Bridegroom's arrival. "And the Spirit and the bride say, 'Come!' Even so, come, Lord Jesus!"[16]

Fresh Anointing for a New Day

IN THIS VERY HOUR IN WHICH WE ARE LIVING, I believe that the Lord is releasing His anointing on His people to a degree unseen since the first century. There is a new sense of urgency. I see God restoring His Church and bringing about a new type of anointing for America. I am seeing greater and greater manifestations of His glory much sooner than I anticipated. We are coming into a new prophetic hour.

When I was in Jerusalem in 1991, the Spirit of God came upon me and began speaking to me about the anointing. He reminded me of Mark 11:22, where Jesus said, "Have faith in God." Then the Lord told me, "Teach people about My anointing. Teach them how to have faith in Me, that I will move mountains for them, and anoint their words in these last days as never before. What they speak will come to pass, because they will be people who carry My anointing."

The Lord wants us not only to experience His anointing, but to learn how to steward it, how to release it, and how to increase it in our lives. He wants to give us spiritual victory, not only as individuals, but as families and as churches. It is critically important that we be alert and ready so that we do not miss our season of divine appointment. He is calling us to welcome His anointing on our lives and to take our place in the most glorious hour and history of the Church.

While it is certainly true that God desires to impart His anointing to us for our own healing and deliverance, there is more. He wants us to be so empowered and energized with the anointing that we become instruments of His miracles; that we will take the anointing with us into the world and break the yokes of bondage, sin, and sickness. The anointing destroys the yoke.[17]

The nations of the earth are famished for the anointing of the Holy Spirit. For too long they have starved on the empty husks of humanism, intellectualism, and false religions. Now they are hungry to see Jesus and His power. We, His Church, are the Bride of Christ, filled, prepared, and anointed to share His life, His light, and His healing power to a desperate and dying world.

The Breath of His Presence

SO, THEN, WHAT EXACTLY IS THE ANOINTING? Simply stated, *the anointing is the power of God manifest in our midst*. It is the breeze of His divine and holy Presence, the very breath of the Spirit. It is the soft, glowing light of the life of Christ shining in us and through us. The anointing is the bubbling overflow from the wellsprings of God—the "rivers of living water" flowing out of our hearts.[18] It is a magnetic quality of character resting on us that attracts people, indescribable yet undeniable. It was just such a quality that made Jesus impossible to dismiss. Jesus walked constantly in the Spirit's anointing and as a result made an impact on everyone He met. Many loved Him, many others hated Him, but no one ignored Him.

The Spirit's anointing draws us to the Word of God, brings it to our remembrance, and opens it up to our understanding, applying it in our hearts for specific situations. It takes the Word (*logos*) of God—the general utterances of God—and makes it the Word (*rhema*) of God for us, bringing it to life in specific and personal application to our circumstances. When we are under the anointing, we are empowered to move and walk in the Spirit and to do the works of Jesus.

The Lord Himself depended on the anointing of the Spirit in order to do the mighty works that He did. Luke records that "on a certain day, as He was teaching…the power of the Lord was present to heal them."[19]

71

The "power of the Lord" was the anointing. If Jesus needed it, how much more, then, do *we* need it!

As we consider the anointing, we need to be careful that we don't overanalyze. Our sophisticated and modern age has taught us to be critical and to scrutinize everything. It seems as though we want to take every thought, every idea, every concept, and dissect it. We do this even to the Word of God. I'm not against careful, thorough study of the Scriptures, but we need to watch out that we don't get so focused on the details that we lose sight of the whole.

Years ago, when I was a pre-med student, I dissected many specimens as part of my studies in anatomy. One thing I realized is that we dissect *dead* things. The Word of God is *alive* and *active*. The Holy Spirit is alive. We cannot dissect them. Instead of trying so hard to dissect and analyze, we should simply come in childlike faith and *receive*. We should relax and let the Lord impart His Spirit and His anointing to us. We should allow Him to fill us and permeate us with the breath of His Presence. Then, as we learn to walk in the anointing, we will find ourselves clothed with power from on high, and the Spirit Himself will lead us into deeper understanding of the "details." Dissection attempts to understand by going from the outside *in*. The anointing gives us understanding from the inside *out*.

The Power of the Anointing

I BELIEVE THAT IN THESE LAST DAYS God is preparing us to do battle the way Moses did. After his encounter with God at the burning bush, Moses returned to Egypt carrying what the Bible calls the "rod of God." By all appearances it was just a piece of wood, a simple shepherd's staff. Yet it was anointed with the miracle-working power of God. Moses carried God's anointing with him. In Egypt, Moses did battle with Pharaoh's magicians. The magicians came up short. When, at Moses' command, his brother Aaron threw down the "rod of God," it turned into a serpent. The Egyptian magicians threw down their staffs also, which, through their dark and magic arts, also became serpents. The "rod of God" ate up the other serpents, however, demonstrating that the powers of darkness are no match for the Lord God Almighty.[20]

Moses had a better rod, a rod anointed with the power of God. Before Moses was through, everyone in Egypt, from the pharaoh on his throne to the slave in the dungeon, knew of the power and the glory of the God of Moses. In our own day, the Lord is anointing His people for miracles, signs, and wonders. He is anointing us to minister healing. He is anointing us to do warfare with the forces of darkness. That's why it is so critical for us to stay plugged into the anointing.

A number of years ago I held a crusade in Hungary. They had rented a sports hall in Budapest, and every night every seat was filled—seven thousand people—with several thousand more standing outside. One night the Lord gave me a word of knowledge that He wanted to minister to those who had attempted suicide. It was a strange word to me, but I had long since learned to obey the Lord's voice. I said, "All of you who have attempted suicide, God wants to heal the wounds in your life and deliver you. Come on up." I expected perhaps a few dozen people to come forward. To my utter amazement, more than 1,200 people came to the front! Later, I was told that the nation of Hungary had one of the highest suicide rates in the world.

Looking out over that sea of 1,200 faces gazing back at me, I was at a loss as to what to do. I prayed frantically, "Lord, here they are; what do I do now?"

The Lord answered, "Welcome My anointing."

So I simply said, "Holy Spirit, come now." As soon as I said that, all 1,200 people at the front fell out at one time under the power of the Spirit. At that moment the yoke was broken and they were all delivered from the spirit of suicide. It was not me. All I did was welcome the Spirit. The anointing—God's power manifest in that place—brought deliverance and healing. That's the power of the anointing.

Focus on the Primary Things

THE LORD WANTS TO FILL US with His power. He wants us to walk in His anointing so He can pour out His love, His blessings, His compassion, and His healing mercy over the world. For most Christians, receiving the anointing is not the problem; the challenge is *keeping* it. We receive the anointing when we come to Jesus in faith and repent of our sins. The Holy Spirit then comes to take up permanent residence in our hearts. As we learn to listen to and obey His voice, and as we are filled with the Spirit, we begin to see more and more evidence of the presence and growth of the anointing in our lives.

Repentance is not a one-time event, however. If we want to stay sharp and in tune with the Spirit, we need to get in the habit of practicing *daily* repentance. The cleaner we are, the more the Lord can use us. The more we keep our sins confessed up to date, the closer and more joyful our fellowship with God will be. How many of us would eat from a dirty dish or drink from a grimy glass? In the same way, the Lord seeks *clean* vessels and *pure* hearts. Confession is not fun. None of us like to admit our faults and weaknesses, not even to God. Confession is vital to our spiritual health and well being, however, and absolutely critical for keeping the anointing.

Keeping the anointing means learning to focus on the primary things. First of all, we need to focus on Jesus Christ. He is our Savior, our Lord, and our all in all. He is the absolute and supreme love of our hearts, above even our spouses or our children. Focusing on Jesus means getting to know Him better and better and growing to love Him more and more.

One of the things that the Spirit is doing in the hearts of believers is restoring our bridal love for Jesus Christ. That's part of His job. A bride in love wants nothing more passionately than to be with her bridegroom. For the bridegroom the feeling is mutual. Did you know that the Lord Jesus wants to be with us even more than we want to be with Him? I don't know about you, but that thought fires up in me a passion to draw closer and just spend time with Him. When we are in tune with the Holy Spirit, He makes us fall in love with Jesus. He reveals Jesus to us, and the more we see of Jesus, the more we will love Him. The Spirit is preparing the Bride for her Bridegroom.

Secondly, we need to focus on the anointing, in the sense of cultivating a personal relationship with the Holy Spirit. We need to get to know Him and welcome Him, and drink daily and deeply of His water of life that bubbles up in our spirit. The Holy Spirit is a Person, coexistent, coeternal, and coequal with God the Father and Christ the Son. The Three are One. This truth is stated beautifully in the ancient Nicene Creed, which many churches recite every Sunday:

> I believe in one God: the Father Almighty, maker of heaven and earth...And in one Lord Jesus Christ, the only begotten Son of God...being of one substance with the Father...And I believe in the Holy Ghost, the Lord, the giver of life, who proceedeth from the Father and the Son, who with the Father and the Son is worshiped and glorified, who spake by the prophets.

The Holy Spirit is the "giver of life," who is to be "worshiped and glorified" along with the Father and the Son. He is the One who raised Jesus from the dead, and He is the One who works in each of our hearts to bring us to faith in Christ. Under the anointing we drink deep draughts of Spirit-water that renew, refresh, and strengthen us, and under the anointing we share that water abundantly with others.

Let's be sure to focus on the primary things. Obedience and allegiance to Jesus as Lord, and a growing personal relationship with the Holy Spirit are critical keys to keeping the anointing. As we learn to flow in the anointing, we will be able to speak in Christ's name against evil and watch it shrivel and die, just as the fig tree withered when Jesus cursed it. The Lord will release miracles into our lives on a day-to-day basis. We will walk in the realm of the supernatural, and yokes will be broken.

Watch Out for Temptation

ONE OF THE SUREST WAYS TO "LOSE" THE ANOINTING is to neglect our personal relationship with the Holy Spirit. If we grieve Him or quench Him by our stubbornness, by gossip, by backbiting other Christians or by other un-Christlike words or actions, the anointing will lift. Unconfessed sin and unholy living will do it too. Yielding to temptation is one of the greatest hindrances we face in keeping the anointing.

After Jesus was baptized in the Jordan River, He faced a period of testing. "Then Jesus, being filled with the Holy Spirit, returned from the

Jordan and was led by the Spirit into the wilderness, being tempted for forty days by the devil."[21] The *Spirit* led Jesus into the wilderness where He was tempted. During those 40 days satan enticed Jesus with appeals to His appetite (turn stones into bread), His ambition (I will give you the kingdoms of the world if you will worship me), and to the misuse of His power (jump from the top of the Temple so the angels will catch you). In each case, Jesus came through with flying colors. He defeated satan with the Word of God and overcame temptation in the strength of the anointing. Finally, after the ordeal was over, "Jesus returned in the power of the Spirit to Galilee."[22]

Jesus was "led by the Spirit" into the wilderness; He came out of the wilderness "in the power of the Spirit." There is a big difference. Jesus' season in the wilderness tested His mettle, proved His character, and focused His mission. It was only then that He went forth "in the power of the Spirit" to carry out His Father's purpose.

Sometimes the Spirit leads us into the wilderness, not to torment us, but to teach us how to follow Him. He allows us to be broken so that He can remold us and shape us into vessels fit for the Master's use. He permits us to be tried and tested, not to see us fall, but in order to show us the power and subtlety of the enemy, the overcoming power of Christ, and our own helplessness and utter dependence on Him for strength and victory. As we learn these lessons (a lifelong process), we grow more and more in the power and anointing of the Lord. It is part of our preparation for carrying the healing anointing of the Lord. Learning to be led by the Spirit is part of our grooming as children of God and as the Bride of Christ. "For as many as are led by the Spirit of God, these are sons of God."[23]

We don't have to hunt for temptation; it will come our way just as surely as the sun will rise tomorrow. Although we shouldn't seek out temptation, neither should we fear it. Instead, as temptations come, we should learn to see them as opportunities to grow stronger in the Lord. After all, He gave us this promise: "No temptation has overtaken you except such as is common to man; but God is faithful, who will not allow you to be tempted beyond what you are able, but with the temptation will also make the way of escape, that you may be able to bear it."[24]

A Heart of Compassion

AFTER JESUS RETURNED FROM THE WILDERNESS, one of the first things He did, according to Luke, was visit the synagogue in Nazareth, where He announced His mission:

The Spirit of the Lord is upon Me,
Because He has anointed Me
To preach the gospel to the poor;
He has sent Me to heal the brokenhearted,
To proclaim liberty to the captives
And recovery of sight to the blind,
To set at liberty those who are oppressed;
To proclaim the acceptable year of the Lord.[25]

The anointing of the Spirit led Jesus to the lost, the poor, the broken, and the hurting. The fuel that fed His ministry was a burning heart of compassion. Everything Jesus did for people was motivated by His compassion. "But when He saw the multitudes, He was moved with compassion for them, because they were weary and scattered, like sheep having no shepherd."[26]

In the same way, anyone who carries the healing anointing must carry also a heart consumed with compassion for those in need. A future day is coming when God will judge the nations, but in this current dispensation of grace, we are His ministers of mercy and His ambassadors of compassion to the world. The spirits of pride, criticism, condemnation, prejudice, legalism, and judmentalism are completely incompatible with the anointing of the Spirit. In order to do the works of Jesus, we must be *like* Jesus. The only way to be like Jesus is to let Him live His resurrection life in us. If you want to carry the healing anointing, cultivate a heart of mercy and compassion.

This is not easy to do because it requires that we die to self. Only the smell of our burning flesh on the altars of our selfishness will release the full fragrance and potency of the anointing. We can't keep the anointing by hoarding it for ourselves. The only way to keep it is to give it away. We need to stop thinking only about what the anointing can do for us, and consider what it can do for others through us. Walking in the anointing leads us outward, away from ourselves, and onto the paths of service and ministry. The Spirit of the Lord is upon us, and He has anointed us to preach, to heal, and to liberate those who are in bondage.

Seven Keys to Increasing in the Anointing

THERE ARE MANY THINGS WE CAN DO to grow in the anointing. I want to give you seven keys that I have learned through my ministry. These are not the only ones, but they form a framework to build upon.

1. *Faithfully proclaim the gospel of Jesus Christ.* This is absolutely fundamental. As we discussed in Chapter Two, the gospel of Jesus Christ is the heart of everything else. Without Christ there is no healing, no anointing, no salvation, and no gospel. If we proclaim "Jesus Christ and Him crucified,"[27] the anointing will flow in power.

2. *Bless Israel.* Galatians 3:13-14 says that Christ died so that the "blessing of Abraham might come upon the Gentiles in Christ Jesus, that we might receive the promise of the Spirit through faith." The "blessing of Abraham" is one way to refer to the anointing of God. How can we expect to receive the blessing of Abraham if we reject the children of Abraham, the Jews? It is vitally important as Christians that we cooperate with and bless God's purposes where Israel and the Jews are concerned. We need to pray for the Jewish people, pray for the peace of Jerusalem, and pray for God to bless Israel.

3. *Bless the poor.* The heart of the Holy Spirit is to bless the poor. Once, when I was in Africa, I announced a special healing and prayer service for the following day and promised to pray for everyone who came. Over 21,000 people showed up. Old people were brought up in wheelbarrows. Many people had been sitting in their own excrements for days. There were people with leprosy, horrible fungus growths on their faces, and other repulsive diseases. As many as 20 percent of those who came had AIDS. I took these precious people in my arms

78

and said "Jesus loves you," and the Holy Spirit came down. I was touching the poor, and the heart of the Holy Spirit is for the poor. Many people were healed and delivered.

4. *Welcome the Holy Spirit daily.* Don't take Him for granted.

5. *Cultivate the character of Christ*: humility, obedience, gentleness, servanthood, self-sacrifice, purity, holiness. These will create an environment in which the Spirit is delighted to remain.

6. *Practice consistent times of prayer and fasting.* There is no substitute for the combined disciplines of prayer and fasting. For a thorough treatment of this subject, I refer you to my book, *The Hidden Power of Prayer and Fasting.*[28]

7. *Speak in tongues regularly, with praise and thanksgiving.* This is a critical lifeline to the heart of God, yet too many Spirit-filled believers neglect it. Don't be one of them. "In everything give thanks; for this is the will of God in Christ Jesus for you."[29]

Once we understand what the anointing is and what it is for, once we have learned to cultivate our personal relationship with the Holy Spirit, and once we have allowed Him to mold us and prepare us in the "wilderness," we will be ready to move on. The training period is finished. Class is over. It is time to move into the miracle dimension!

Endnotes

1. Zech. 4:6b.

2. Acts 1:8a.

3. 1 Cor. 3:16.

4. 2 Kings 13:20-21.

5. 2 Kings 2:1-2.

6. See 2 Kings 2:3-6.

7. See 2 Kings 2:8.

8. 2 Kings 2:9-11.

9. See 2 Kings 2:19-22.

10. See 2 Kings 4:1-7.

11. See 2 Kings 4:8-17.

12. See 2 Kings 4:32-37.

13. See 2 Kings 4:38-44.

14. See 2 Kings 5:8-14.

15. Rev. 21:2,9-11a.

16. Rev. 22:17a,20b.

17. Is. 10:27b, paraphrased.

18. See Jn. 7:38.

19. Lk. 5:17.

20. See Ex. 7:8-12.

21. Lk. 4:1-2a.

22. Lk. 4:14a.

23. Rom. 8:14.

24. 1 Cor. 10:13.

25. Lk. 4:18-19.

26. Mt. 9:36.

27. 1 Cor. 2:2b.

28. Mahesh Chavda, *The Hidden Power of Prayer and Fasting* (Shippensburg, PA: Destiny Image Publishers, Inc., 1998).

29. 1 Thess. 5:18.

Part Two

Walking in the
Healing Anointing

Chapter Six

Entering the Miracle Dimension

A S WE MAKE OUR WAY down the river, it is very easy to become so comfortable and so self-satisfied that we don't want to do anything to "rock the boat." It's also easy to get so caught up with our own journey that we forget we are not alone. All we have to do is look around to see that we are part of a vast host of voyagers, all traveling downstream in our separate little boats. Some folks are in their "Pentecostal" boat; others, their "Baptist" boat, or their "Methodist," "Presbyterian," "Episcopalian," or "Catholic" boat. Some boats are stately yachts of "tradition," while others are sassy speedboats of the unconventional, darting in and out among the other boats, kicking up waves wherever they go. Strangely enough, there are even a number of boats that are laboring to make their way *upstream*, against the flow of the current!

While a bold few have ventured into midstream, where the current is the strongest, the vast majority of boats stay close to shore, hugging the riverbank. Along the riverbank, watching as this great flotilla sails by, are the millions who have not yet even begun the journey. Many boats come and go, stopping along the bank to talk to those who are on the shore. Afterwards, many of those standing at the water's edge launch out into the stream in little boats of their own. In this way, the fleet grows ever larger.

The Hidden Power of the Believer's Touch

All of us who claim the name of Christ are on the same journey together in the river of God. We progress in different ways and at different speeds according to our background, circumstances, traditions, understanding, and maturity. If we are in Christ, we are all headed in the same direction. Most Christians are content to stay close to shore, where the current is gentler and the challenges smaller. There are others, however, who have a boldness about them—some might even say a "reckless" streak—who are not satisfied with being anywhere other than midstream. They possess a thirst, a drive to press forward for the fullness of God, regardless of the risks.

We can never experience the *fullness* of God's purpose and power until we are willing to put our "boat" squarely in the middle of the current, allowing it to be drawn along by the flow of the Spirit. Sometimes, in fact, the Lord even challenges us to *get out of the boat* and plunge directly into His flow. For many of us, that means entering a whole new dimension of our walk of faith.

A Cup of Water for the Bread of Life

L IKE ALL OF US AT ONE TIME OR ANOTHER, I once was one of those who stood on the riverbank watching the boats go by. I was safe, high and dry on the shore of Hinduism until one day one of those boats came in. My family was descended from an aristocratic Hindu background. We could trace our ancestry by name back eight hundred years in the past. For many generations my ancestors ruled in a certain province in India. My father worked for the British government in Kenya, Africa, but we were committed Hindus. We believed in Shiva, Brahma, and Vishnu; we believed in reincarnation; we believed in the caste system—the whole bit. As I grew older, however, the only thing I knew was that there was no remedy for the sin in our lives. Hinduism has no answer for sin.

I was brought up to know all the holy books of India, and was trained to seek after truth. In fact, I prided myself on being a searcher for truth. All of us want to know the truth. I have never met anyone anywhere who said, "I want lies." We all want the truth. God put a hunger in me to know the truth, and I searched for it aggressively. Many times I walked miles to the Hindu temple, where I talked to the priests and rang the ceremonial bells, but I always left empty. I would come out of the temple and pray, "God, where are You? Show me Your truth. I know You're not in the temple. How can I find You?"

The "boat" that touched my life arrived one day during my high school years. There was a knock on our door, and when I opened it, a Southern Baptist missionary was standing there. She had come to sing some songs to children in the area, and had gotten thirsty. She asked me for a drink of water. When I gave it to her, she gave me a copy of the New Testament. As soon as she left, I started reading it.

It was the most unusual book I had ever read, because I felt like the author was right there in the room, speaking directly to me. That's the way the Bible is. It is different from any other book. Once you start to read it sincerely, the Author Himself will come and start talking to you. As I read, the words came alive to me. The Bible says, "For the word of God is living and powerful, and sharper than any two-edged sword, piercing even to the division of soul and spirit, and of joints and marrow, and is a discerner of the thoughts and intents of the heart."[1] Psalm 107 says that when the people were in distress, "...they cried out to the Lord in their trouble, and He saved them out of their distresses. He sent His word and healed them, and delivered them from their destructions."[2]

As I read further, I came to the place where Jesus said, "I am the way, the truth, and the life. No one comes to the Father except through Me."[3] These words came to life for me. I was looking for truth, and suddenly it seemed as though scales fell off of my eyes, for I saw that truth is a *Person*: Jesus Christ. I also realized immediately that it was not enough simply to say, "Yes, Jesus is the truth"; I had to *receive* that truth personally into my life. I knew that this truth had the power to give eternal life; that in receiving Jesus, He could heal me body, soul, and spirit.

Paying the Price for Eternal Life

IT WAS THEN THAT MY OWN TRADITIONS, background, and culture rose up inside me, telling me, "You have your own way," but in my heart I knew Jesus was the way. I knew I had to receive Him personally. Many weeks passed, however, before I made that decision, because I knew I would be rejected by my family and friends. In my entire ancestry going back eight hundred years, I would be the first one ever to receive Jesus Christ.

I remember reading the Bible one night and saying, "I don't think I can go on anymore; I just can't pay the price." Then I started crying. My head hit the table and I went to sleep, and yet in a way, I was awake. I was taken to a place I'd never been before and found myself walking on streets of gold. I heard the most wonderful music—psalms that put me in perfect ecstasy. I was so happy that I wanted to stay there all my life.

Suddenly, I saw a light coming toward me that was brighter than ten thousand suns put together. It was a strange light, for it did not hurt my eyes. In the midst of that light I saw Jesus. I will never forget His eyes. In His eyes I saw all the pain and suffering that anyone could endure. It seemed as though He had cried every tear that had ever been shed, and yet His eyes shone with limitless happiness, joy, and laughter. He was full of victory. He came towards me, put His hand on my shoulder, and said, "My little brother." Then I woke up.

It was nine o'clock in the evening when I had gone to sleep, and I woke up when the roosters crowed around four o'clock the following morning. Upon waking up I discovered that my Bible was open to a place where it had not been opened before—chapter 18 of Luke, where the rich young ruler comes to the Lord and walks away sad because the price of following Jesus was too great to pay. Then the Lord asked me, "Are you going to be the same way?"

I said, "No, Sir," and got down on my knees, repented of my sins, and received Jesus Christ as my Savior and my Lord. I realized I was the first one of all my ancestry who had ever known what it was to be forgiven of his sins and to be washed in the blood of Jesus. It was the greatest experience! At that moment I stepped off the shore of Hinduism and launched my little boat into the river of God.

When I got off my knees, I knew that I had eternal life and that I was going to go to Heaven! Jesus had put supernatural life in me, and I felt like Superman! I wanted to go stop trains and leap over tall buildings in a single bound! *I had eternal life!*

Discovering the Spirit as the Power for Life

AFTER HIGH SCHOOL I came to the United States to attend a Bible college, where I received my bachelor's degree. I started graduate studies at Texas Tech University. While I was there, I received the news that my mother, who was living in England then, was dying of a terminal illness and wanted to see me before she died. My mother was in England and I was a poor graduate student in Texas; I had no money to go see her. She was dying and I felt helpless and hopeless.

During my years of school in the United States, I had gotten very proud of my intellectualism and had slowly drifted away from the Lord and the Church. At the news of my mother's condition, I cried for three days because I had no answer either for her or for myself. I had come to the end of my resources.

Actually, that's not so bad a place to be, because when we reach the end of our resources we find Jesus Christ there ready to take over. Our sinful nature makes us reluctant to release our situation to the Lord entirely; we want to insist that we can still handle our affairs by ourselves. God is asking us now for *complete* and *absolute surrender*. When we do surrender to Him, He can do great things through us, but not as long as we have one foot in the world and the other in the Kingdom of God.

On that third night I cried myself to sleep, expecting that my mother would die any day now and that I would never see her again. In my sleep I found myself in the same place where I had been many years before, walking the streets of gold. Then I moved to a grassy area, where I knelt down. Jesus was tending to me with His hands on my shoulders. I was looking into His face and singing in a language I could not understand.

When I woke up, I knew I had been with Jesus, and had a strong desire to pray. As I began praying, a wind blew into my room and snapped the door open. The wind seemed to surround me, and I felt something bubbling up inside. I opened my mouth and a song came out.

87

Now, I knew English and I knew Gujarati, an Indian dialect, and some Swahili. I even knew a little German, but the language I was singing was none of those. It was completely different. The intellectual side of me—the side that was a graduate student—said, "This is *weird!*" The rest of me said, "Shut up! This is the most wonderful thing I've ever experienced, and I'm going to sing some more!" Then I opened my mouth and sang in this new language.

Although I didn't understand what had happened, I did know that Jesus was more alive and real to me than He had ever been before. At that time, the only spiritual person I knew in graduate school was a Catholic nun. So, on Monday I explained what had happened to me, then asked her, "Sister Marsha, am I going crazy?" She put her books down, looked at me, and started jumping up and down. Then she said, "Praise God, brother, you've been baptized in the Holy Spirit!"

Over the next few weeks the Holy Spirit became very real to me. I started speaking and praying regularly in this new language, and the Spirit of God began speaking to my spirit. He said, "Jesus is the same yesterday, today and forever." I said, "Yes." He repeated it twice more, and I asked, "Lord, what are You trying to say?"

He said, "Pray for your mother and I will heal her."

"Lord," I answered, "she's in England and I'm in Texas."

He said, "You pray. I am the Healer."

So, I prayed. A few weeks later I got a letter informing me that my mother was completely healed. That was nearly 30 years ago. My mother lived another 24 years in good health, and in the meantime this precious Hindu woman found Christ.

Training in the School of the Spirit

I WAS NOW "ENROLLED" IN THE SCHOOL OF THE SPIRIT, and He began training me in the ways of the Lord. The Bible says in Romans, "For as many as are led by the Spirit of God, these are sons of God."[4] As the Spirit leads us, we grow into maturity as sons and daughters of the King.

Under the Spirit's guiding, I came to understand the pattern in which He works. Jesus' own experience is the perfect illustration. After He was baptized in the Jordan River, the Spirit *led* Jesus into the wilderness, where He confronted and defeated satan through prayer, fasting, and the Word of God. Then Jesus came out of the wilderness in the *power* of the Spirit and began His public ministry. Jesus described His ministry by saying, "The Spirit of the Lord is upon Me, because He has anointed me..."[5]

The anointing of the Spirit is the key, the secret behind the power of the ministry of Jesus. All His preaching and teaching, as well as His healings and other miracles were done under the anointing of the Holy Spirit. By His own life, Jesus has given us an example: The Spirit led Him into the wilderness; He came out in the power of the Spirit, and ministered under the anointing of the Spirit.

After I was filled with the Spirit and He started guiding me, He gave me a word: "I'm sending you as My ambassador of love." I said, "Yes, Lord." He then led me to work at a state school for mentally handicapped children. These were severely needy children whose parents either could not or would not care for, and so were wards of the state. Many of them were blind or deaf, or profoundly handicapped, some to the extent that they never got out of their beds. The Lord said to me, "I love them. In My Word I have promised to take care of those forsaken by their mother and father. I am sending you as My ambassador to love these little ones."

I worked with these children hours at a time. Some could not even sit up on their own. Others were physically adults—20 years old but with the mind of a two-year-old. I remember sitting in a chair, just holding them in my arms and praying in the Spirit, and the Lord started healing them. It took me completely by surprise. A little girl who had been born blind started seeing; a boy who had never walked started walking. I discovered for myself that God really *is* a God of love, and that He wants to use us as His ambassadors, to minister His love to the hurting, the poor, and the broken lives around us. Healing is *His* responsibility; ours is to be open to the leading of His Spirit.

Are You Thirsty?

IN THIS DAY AND HOUR the Spirit of God wants to raise up an army of men and women who will receive His infilling, and who will allow Him to lead them. Everyone must begin at the same place—receiving Jesus Christ as Savior and Lord. The next step is to be filled with the Spirit. In John chapter 7, Jesus said, "If anyone thirsts, let him come to Me and drink. He who believes in Me, as the Scripture has said, out of his heart will flow rivers of living water."[6] The next verse explains that the "rivers of living water" refers to the Holy Spirit.

On the Day of Pentecost, when certain people in the crowd in Jerusalem asked Simon Peter, "What shall we do?" he answered, "Repent, and let every one of you be baptized in the name of Jesus Christ for the remission of sins; and you shall receive the gift of the Holy Spirit."[7] We repent by turning our backs on our sin and on satan and his kingdom of darkness, and receiving Jesus as Savior and Lord. Then, as we yield to Him and obey Him, He will fill us with the Holy Spirit.

This is the Lord's desire for all of His children—you, me, and every other believer. To receive it, however, we must be *thirsty*. Jesus invited all who were *thirsty* to go to Him and drink. We must be thirsty for more of God. What kind of thirst is that? It's the kind of thirst you would have if you had gone through a desert for three days without a drink of water. Think how *desperate* you would be for a drink! You would be willing to do *anything* to get it. It's the kind of thirst in which we are desperate for more of Jesus. He fills us according to the degree of our thirst. The thirstier we are, the more abundant is His filling. Jesus didn't say that He would give us a cup of water, but that *rivers* of living water would flow from within.

The End-Times Bride Adorned for Her Husband

OUR THIRST FOR GOD could also be likened to the longing a new bride feels for her husband, or a bridegroom for his wife, especially if they are separated from one another. Those of you who are married, do you remember how you felt in those earliest days of marriage? How anxious you were to be with your spouse and how you ached inside when you were apart?

That's the way we believers as the Bride of Christ should feel toward our Bridegroom. In the words of the apostle John, we, the Church, are "the holy city, New Jerusalem, coming down out of heaven from God, prepared as a bride adorned for her husband."[8] Christ is our Bridegroom. We should long for His presence and eagerly look forward to being reunited with Him. Our hearts should anxiously desire His coming: "And the Spirit and the bride say, 'Come!' And let him who hears say, 'Come!' And let him who thirsts come. Whoever desires, let him take the water of life freely."[9]

I believe that we are the end-time generation of the Church. So many prophecies of the endtimes are being fulfilled all around us, especially those dealing with the nation of Israel. Even though we have been in the "last days" since the Day of Pentecost, I believe that we are seeing in our own generation, as never before, the fulfillment of the ancient prophecy:

> *And it shall come to pass in the last days, says God, that I will pour out of My Spirit on all flesh; your sons and your daughters shall prophesy, your young men shall see visions, your old men shall dream dreams. And on My menservants and on My maidservants I will pour out My Spirit in those days; and they shall prophesy. I will show wonders in heaven above and signs in the earth beneath: blood and fire and vapor of smoke. The sun shall be turned into darkness, and the moon into blood, before the coming of the great and awesome day of the Lord. And it shall come to pass that whoever calls on the name of the Lord shall be saved.*[10]

One of the last and most glorious assignments the Holy Spirit has on earth is to prepare the Bride of Christ to be ushered into the presence of the Bridegroom. Part of that preparation is to present her with gifts to wear—gifts that are fit for the Bride of the King of Heaven. The greatest gift is the Spirit Himself, who indwells the Church. However, the indwelling Spirit manifests Himself in a garland of end-time gifts that adorns the neck of the Bride: the gifts of prophecy and healing, of miracles and signs and wonders, of words of knowledge and words of wisdom, and of tongues and interpretation of tongues. The Bride of Christ will be recognized by her gifts and by her glory, because she will be equally yoked with her Bridegroom, the Lord of glory.

The "Eight-Cow Woman"

THERE IS A STORY THAT COMES FROM THE POLYNESIAN ISLANDS about a young tradesman who was quite successful in his business, becoming the wealthiest man in the area. He fell in love with a young woman and wanted to marry her. According to the custom in Polynesia, a man who desired to marry would go to the girl's father and give him a gift in exchange for her hand in marriage. If the woman was beautiful and the man desired her desperately, the common gift was a cow. If she was extraordinarily lovely, the gift might be two cows. If she was "moderate" in her looks, the standard gift was a goat. If she *really* needed help, her suitor could win her hand by giving her father a few chickens.

The rich young tradesman fell in love with a young maiden who was one of the plainest-looking women in all of Polynesia. Her father probably would have accepted a single chicken—or even a single *egg*—for her. According to custom, as the oldest daughter she had to be married before her more attractive younger sister could be wed. She needed a husband, but her prospects were not very good until the young tradesman came along. He approached her father with a proposal of marriage and offered his gift. The father, hoping for *maybe* a goat, but willing to settle for a chicken, was astounded when the young man presented him with *eight cows*! Such an extravagant gift was unheard of, even for the most ravishingly beautiful woman!

When asked why he gave such an extraordinary gift for the woman, the young man answered, "I love her. To me, she is the most beautiful woman in the world." According to Polynesian history, that woman, knowing she was loved and prized so highly by her husband, actually *became* the most beautiful woman in all of Polynesia. Her husband paid the highest price for her. She was the "eight-cow woman."

Jesus is the Bridegroom. For us, He paid the most expensive price ever paid in the history of the universe. He shed His precious blood for His Bride. We are His Bride, highly esteemed and special to Him. In His eyes, we are the "eight-cow woman," and He wants to make us beautiful and fill us with His glory.

Entering the Supernatural Realm

THE CHURCH IS THE BRIDE OF CHRIST. We are the dearly beloved of His heart, for whom He died, and in this end-time generation His Spirit is adorning us in preparation for our entering into the supernatural realm—the dimension of miracles, signs, and wonders. In our day and hour the Lord is pouring out His Spirit on His people in a visitation unlike anything the Church has seen since Pentecost. In my ministry all over the world I am seeing vast numbers of young people who are hungry for God getting filled with the power of the Spirit. That which is happening in other parts of the world can also happen right here in America. God is doing wonderful things in the hearts and lives of our children, and He desires to do the same thing in our hearts and lives. The Lord wants us to enter the miracle dimension. He has invited us to step into the supernatural realm.

That realm is the dimension of the Spirit. It is the realm of the glory of the Lamb, a realm that we cannot really understand or relate to theologically. We must relate to it spirit to Spirit. We must walk into that realm by faith. God is increasing signs and wonders all over the world, in America as well as in Africa. This is the hour for you and me and our children to enter in. The Lord wants the miracle dimension to be no longer only theoretical for us, but *experiential*. Once we taste the glory of the presence of the Lord, it will become a sweet and glorious addiction for us. We will constantly want more and more of His presence and His glory because we can't get enough of Him. It's the most wonderful addiction anyone could have.

Some time ago when I was in Los Angeles, I visited Azusa Street, where the modern Pentecostal movement was born. The old warehouse where the Spirit fell a century ago is today the location of a Japanese cultural center. However, it was wonderful to walk there and think about how a one-eyed black preacher named William Seymour preached there, but more often, simply fell on his face and sought the Lord in weeping and prayer.

Because of the prayers of this black brother, the glory of God descended on Azusa Street and, as a result, thousands of people received the filling of the Holy Spirit. The Presence of God came down, the fire of the Spirit went out, and multitudes of people were healed and delivered. The glory was so awesome that it is said that policemen would come within six or seven blocks of that Azusa Street warehouse and suddenly be hit by the power of God, fall, and be unable to come any further. God wants to put that kind of power in each one of us. His glory is not limited to an elite group of "super saints"; He intends it for all of us.

I once visited the grave of Charles Finney. When this great nineteenth-century revivalist preached, hundreds of thousands came to the Lord. Finney's ministry was accompanied by dramatic and powerful manifestations of the Spirit. For example, there were times when Finney would simply enter a city, and the presence of God was so strong that people would get off their horses in the streets and start crying and repenting before the Lord. Finney would enter a warehouse or factory, and immediately everyone in the building would be slain in the Spirit. It is a documented fact that when Finney preached in Rochester, New York, revival fell, and not a single crime was recorded in the city for the next six months!

That's the power that comes when the Spirit falls. It's the same power that the Lord wants to fill each of us with, so that we will be a holy army full of the glory of God. I believe the day is coming when "ordinary" saints like you and me will be so filled with the presence and glory of the Lord that we will walk into places like K-Mart or the mall, and people will fall over from the power of the Spirit.

Man Overboard!

IN ORDER TO ENTER THIS REALM of supernatural power and the miracle dimension, we must be prepared in faith to step outside the bounds of the conventional and the ordinary, looking for God to do the unconventional and the extraordinary in and through us. The apostle Peter got a brief taste of this potential one stormy night on the Sea of Galilee. After the miracle of feeding the five thousand, Peter and the other disciples had set out to cross the lake while Jesus dismissed the multitudes. Jesus then went up a mountain alone to pray. Meanwhile, the boat was caught in contrary winds and tossed by the waves.

> *Now in the fourth watch of the night Jesus went to them, walking on the sea. And when the disciples saw Him walking on the sea, they were troubled, saying, "It is a ghost!" And they cried out for fear. But immediately Jesus spoke to them, saying, "Be of good cheer! It is I; do not be afraid." And Peter answered Him and said, "Lord, if it is You, command me to come to You on the water." So He said, "Come." And when Peter had come down out of the boat, he walked on the water to go to Jesus. But when he saw that the wind was boisterous, he was afraid; and beginning to sink he cried out, saying, "Lord, save me!" And immediately Jesus stretched out His hand and caught him, and said to him, "O you of little faith, why did you doubt?" And when they got into the boat, the wind ceased. Then those who were in the boat came and worshiped Him, saying, "Truly You are the Son of God."[11]*

Jesus walked in the dimension of glory. When that glory was present, Jesus could walk on land or water—it didn't matter. When Peter saw Jesus walking on the water toward them, he asked, "Lord, if it is You, command me to come to You on the water." It took a lot of faith for Peter to ask that of the Lord. However, it required even more faith for him to step out of the boat when Jesus said, "Come."

Peter jumped overboard and into the miracle dimension. As long as he focused on Jesus he was fine; he walked on the water. As soon as the practical and rational side of him reasserted itself, however, he began to sink. He took his eyes off Jesus and focused on the "realities" of the wind and waves. "What am I doing? I can't walk on water! Help, Lord!"

Even though he floundered, Peter was willing to get out of the boat. Although in this instance it was only for a few seconds, he entered the miracle dimension. Much later, after Pentecost, Peter raised the dead and many sick people who came within his shadow were healed.

Step Out of the Boat!

JUST AS JESUS SAID TO PETER, "COME," that windy night on the Sea of Galilee, so He extends to us the same invitation. "Come. In faith, step out of the boat into My presence, into the anointing, into the realm of glory." The Lord gave me a prophetic word once. He said, "Tell My people, 'Go overboard.' " Many believers are afraid to go overboard. They don't want to get out of their comfortable, secure boat. Those who have a hunger to enter the miracle dimension have to be willing to step out of the boat.

Jesus Himself is starting to rock some of our boats because He wants to give us a revelation of Himself. The same things Jesus did, the apostles did, and we will do if we allow Him to draw us into the realm of glory. "Most assuredly, I say to you, he who believes in Me, the works that I do he will do also; and greater works than these he will do, because I go to My Father."[12] He wants us to step out of the boat and enter the miracle dimension. It doesn't matter what it looks like out there, how gusty the wind or boisterous the waves. He is telling us, "Come. Simply step out of the boat. Don't be afraid. You're not alone; I'm already out here."

When we step out into that other dimension, we do not change. We are still the same people we always have been. But the atmosphere around us is crackling with God's electricity. God's will is to bless us in order to make us a blessing to others. When we enter the miracle dimension by faith, the Spirit's anointing flows through us. It doesn't matter what our background is or how much education we have. It doesn't matter how old we are, whether we are male or female, or whether we are black, white, brown, yellow, or red. God says to all of us, "Come. You are the glorious Bride of Christ. Come into this glorious realm and let Me make you a reservoir of My glory!"

Are you willing to pay the price? What do you want? The safety and security of the boat, or the adventure and wonder of the miracle dimension? The apostles were just as ordinary as we are. What made the difference for them? They simply believed Jesus and were filled with His Spirit. If we believe Jesus and are filled with His Spirit, we can expect to walk in the same ways as Jesus and the disciples did, and see Him do the same kinds of things in and through us.

Jesus is extending His hand and saying, "Come." *Are you willing to step out of the boat?*

Endnotes

1. Heb. 4:12.

2. Ps. 107:19-20.

3. Jn. 14:6.

4. Rom. 8:14.

5. Lk. 4:18.

6. Jn. 7:37b-38.

7. Acts 2:38.

8. Rev. 21:2b.

9. Rev. 22:17.

10. Acts 2:17-21.

11. Mt. 14:25-33.

12. Jn. 14:12.

Chapter Seven

Developing Healing Ministries

B EFORE WE CAN ENTER THE MIRACLE DIMENSION of signs and wonders, or begin to develop healing ministries, or begin to teach people, we must first ask ourselves a fundamental question: *Am I satisfied with my life and ministry, or do I want more of Jesus?* This is a very important question, because we can easily become self-satisfied, and the Lord generally leaves the self-satisfied alone. He responds eagerly, however, to the hungry and the thirsty—to anyone who is *desperate* for Him. Elisha was desperate for a double portion of Elijah's anointing, so he would not leave the prophet's side. Peter was so hungry for the Lord that he jumped out of the boat to walk to Jesus on the water. Like Elisha and Peter, we have to be hungry enough to keep pressing in and saying, "Lord, I want more. Whatever You are doing on earth, I want to be right in the middle of it with You!"

Are you that hungry? If you are reading this book, I assume that you want more of God—that you crave a "double portion" of His anointing on your life. You sense something within, the drawing of God's Spirit impelling you to press in deeper. I believe that if you have gotten this far, you are ready to jump overboard and plunge into the river of God, and to learn how to let His rivers of living water flow out of your life.

Jesus Has Commissioned Us

AT THE OUTSET, we need to remember that in the work of the King-dom of God we *never* act on our own authority. Our authority comes from Christ Himself, who received His authority from the Father. We looked at this matter of authority in Chapter Four, but it bears repeating here. Jesus never acted on His own, but only under the authority and anointing of His Father. In turn, Jesus has commissioned us to act under His authority. Don't forget that Jesus said, "All authority has been given to Me...Go therefore and make disciples..."[1], and "Go into all the world and preach the gospel....And these signs will follow..."[2]

John recorded another "commission" that Jesus issued to His followers.

Then, the same day at evening, being the first day of the week, when the doors were shut where the disciples were assembled, for fear of the Jews, Jesus came and stood in the midst, and said to them, "Peace be with you." When He had said this, He showed them His hands and His side. Then the disciples were glad when they saw the Lord. So Jesus said to them again, "Peace to you! As the Father has sent Me, I also send you." And when He had said this, He breathed on them, and said to them, "Receive the Holy Spirit."[3]

Jesus' disciples had locked themselves away out of fear of the Jews. Fear is one weapon satan uses to keep the people of God from engaging the needs of suffering humanity. Another is to lock us into a system of tradition and unbelief that limits the Word of God and makes it of no effect in our lives. Satan also tries to limit us by challenging our identity and self-esteem. "Who do you think you are, trying to serve the Lord? You're *nobody*; no gifts, no talents, no training, no education, no poten-tial, and no future."

Despite his lies, one thing satan cannot do is remove the destiny and calling that God has placed upon His people. Jesus came to His disciples, calmed their fears, and then gave them His commission: "As the Father has sent Me, I also send you." He backed up His authority by imparting to them the power to act on it: "And when He had said this, He breathed on them, and said to them, 'Receive the Holy Spirit.'"

Jesus' commission is still in force today. All of us who are believers in this generation are heirs of His authority and legacy. For us, His Word is still alive, active, and full of power. Wherever Jesus went, miracles happened: Cripples walked, blind people saw, broken hearts healed, and dead people came back to life. When we go out under the authority and name of Jesus and in the power of His Spirit, we can expect to see similar things, particularly in this end-time generation.

Any time we feel discouraged by our own weaknesses or daunted by the magnitude of the needs and suffering before us, it's good to be able to return and remember our commission: "As the Father has sent Me, I also send you." We don't have to be strong, because *He* is strong! We don't have to be powerful, because *He* is powerful! We don't have to be wise, because *He* is wise! We don't have to *be* anything, because *He is everything!* All we have to do is trust and obey. Let's remember our commission.

Jesus Is Our Model for Proclaiming the Gospel With Authority

HOW DO WE CARRY OUT OUR COMMISSION? What model do we use as a pattern for our life and ministry? There is only one model: Jesus Christ. "As the Father has sent Me, I also send you." As men and women of God, we are called to follow after Jesus.

If we study the life of Jesus, we find that wherever He went preaching the gospel, healings and deliverances from evil spirits also occurred. In everything He did, Jesus spoke and acted with great authority. For example, consider this account from the Gospel of Mark:

Now after John was put in prison, Jesus came to Galilee, preaching the gospel of the kingdom of God, and saying, "The time is fulfilled, and the kingdom of God is at hand. Repent, and believe in the gospel."...Then they went into Capernaum, and immediately on the Sabbath He entered the synagogue and taught. And they were astonished at His teaching, for He taught them as one having authority, and not as the scribes.[4]

101

The Hidden Power of the Believer's Touch

Jesus came preaching the gospel of the Kingdom of God. He said, "The time is fulfilled, and the kingdom of God is at hand. Repent, and believe in the gospel." Jesus had a sense that wherever He was, the Kingdom of God was present. He wants to develop in us that same sense of awareness. Each of us is a little "colony" of Heaven, because we carry His Kingdom and His presence with us wherever we go.

I did a crusade once in Haiti, a nation that was steeped in voodoo and devastated by poverty. Poor, hungry, and malnourished people were everywhere. Yet, none of this existed within the compound of the United States embassy in Haiti. The embassy was a little colony of America, and as such reflected the health, wealth, and overall prosperity of our nation.

In the same manner, we are ambassadors of the Lord Jesus Christ, and wherever we are, the Kingdom of God is present. Just as Jesus preached repentance and faith, so should we help lead people into a walk of repentance. It's vitally important that as people see the Kingdom of God in us, they are moved to repent and believe the gospel.

Jesus always spoke with authority. This was unusual because in His day, it was customary for rabbis to authenticate their teaching by appealing to the teachings and commentary of great rabbis of the past. Jesus, however, spoke on His *own* authority, and this astonished His listeners.

Whenever the Kingdom of God is present in power, it is accompanied by an undeniable sense of authority. Many times, people don't understand it and can't explain it, but neither can they deny it. I have witnessed this time and time again, particularly in my overseas crusades. The forces of darkness simply cannot stand in the face of the power and authority of Jesus.

Jesus Is Our Model for Ministering Healing and Deliverance

EVERY TIME JESUS SPOKE or ministered in authority, the demonic realm was shaken. Look at what happens next in Mark's account.

Now there was a man in their synagogue with an unclean spirit. And he cried out, saying, "Let us alone! What have we to do with You, Jesus of Nazareth? Did You come to destroy us? I know who You are—the Holy One of God!" But Jesus rebuked him, saying, "Be quiet, and come out of him!" And when the unclean spirit had convulsed him and cried out with a loud voice, he came out of him. Then they were all amazed, so that they questioned among themselves, saying, "What is this? What new doctrine is this? For with authority He commands even the unclean spirits, and they obey Him." And immediately His fame spread throughout all the region around Galilee.[5]

Jesus' holy presence in the synagogue stirred up the unholy spirit residing in one of the men present. Jesus didn't play around with that demon. He didn't counsel him, He didn't soften His words; and He didn't beat around the bush. He simply commanded him to leave: "Be quiet, and come out of him!" In our way of speaking today, that would be, "Shut up, and get out!" The unclean spirit shut up and got out. He had no choice; this was the Son of God talking! *That's authority!*

In this hour, in every city in the United States, in every city in the world, in every nation, there are hundreds of millions of people who are under the yoke of demonic oppression. It may be witchcraft or idol worship, sexual lust or perversion. It may be depression and thoughts of suicide, or drug or alcohol addiction.

The answer for these people does not lie in some kind of religious statement, or in some government program birthed in our nation's capital. It isn't found in some political movement, or in psychological counseling. The only answer is deliverance from the yoke of evil spirits, and the only people authorized to administer that deliverance are those who make up the Church of Jesus Christ, and who represent His Kingdom on earth.

Delivered From the Spirit of Witchcraft

ONCE, WHEN I WAS HOLDING A BIG CRUSADE in Costa Rica, some of the pastors sponsoring the crusade asked me to minister in one of the finest churches in the nation. It was a very proper, staid church where the high society went, and normally did not move in the kind of ministry that

I have. I didn't think it was a good idea for me to go, because I was afraid that my ministry would create problems for the pastor of that church, and I didn't want to do that. When the others assured me that this pastor had made the request himself, I agreed to talk with him.

When we sat down together, I was very honest with him. "You know," I said, "it would be better for me not to come, because if I come I won't hold back."

He said to me, "Brother Mahesh, my people are *dead*; you won't hurt them!"

Then I said, "Now *that's* a *great* invitation!" So, I went and ministered at his church. I *tried* to behave myself, I really did. I *tried* to be all staid and proper and everything. I even preached a nice, proper sermon. At the end, however, the ushers suddenly started falling down left and right. I said, "Well, I think the Holy Spirit is here to minister to the people. If you need healing, come on up."

People started coming, they started falling down, and the Lord started healing. At one point, the pastor brought to me an attractive, well-dressed woman who was a member of a leading family in the city. Her nine-year-old son was with her. She had told the pastor in Spanish, "I don't believe in this Jesus, but my son is afraid to go out, and he's afraid to go to school. He's so full of fear; can this man pray for him?"

The woman was standing before me with her son in front of her. The pastor said simply, "This boy has fear."

I said, "All right," and stretched out my hand, but my hand didn't go out to the boy, but to his mother. Then I said, "You demon of witchcraft, come out of this woman now in Jesus' name!"

Suddenly she stepped back, her face contorted like a cobra, and her tongue shot out of her mouth farther than I had ever seen a human tongue come out. She looked like a lizard taking flies. All the people around her started to scatter, but I just looked at her and laughed, and said, "Satan, you know your day is up. Get out of her now!" Then she shook and fell back onto the floor.

I looked at the pastor, whose eyes were wide open with amazement, and said, "Now, finish this."

He said, "Me?"

I said, "Yes, lead her to the Lord." Then I went to pray for others.

A few minutes later, I heard the most beautiful singing in the Spirit. I turned around and saw this beautiful woman in her gorgeous dress and diamonds still lying on the floor, weeping, her mascara running down her face. The pastor had led her to confess Jesus Christ as Savior, and the Lord had sovereignly filled her with the Spirit. She was singing in tongues, baptized in the Spirit, and completely delivered. That day deliverance came to her entire family.

Changed Forever in Two Minutes

A S THE FATHER SENT JESUS, Jesus is sending us. He is our model. Jesus often combined healing and deliverance. As we carry out our commission to do the works of Jesus, we also will often see healing combined with deliverance. There is no adventure more exciting than to go into this field of doing the works of Jesus Christ, and ministering rivers of living water to others. In a matter of a few moments you can see the eternal destiny of people change before your eyes. Bondages that have held people in torment for years are broken in seconds as they encounter the power of the living God, and they are set free.

I remember when a family brought their 40-year-old daughter to me for prayer. The daughter had spent half her life in one mental institution after another. She seemed driven to take her own life. Once she had tried to drown herself in the ocean. She had permanent scars from the third-degree burns she suffered after pouring gasoline on herself and igniting it. She had been under the care of one psychiatrist after another, and was under constant medication.

As I met with this family to pray for their daughter, the Lord gave me a word of knowledge, and revealed to me that an evil spirit was tormenting her. I commanded that evil spirit to come out of her in Jesus' name. The spirit departed. Today, this woman is leading a normal life, working a steady job, and has not needed any further institutionalization. She has been completely delivered. In a matter of two minutes, her life was changed forever by the power of the Lord Jesus Christ.

The Gospel Is to be *Seen* as Well as Heard

ONE FACT THAT COMES OUT CLEARLY in the New Testament is that the gospel of Jesus Christ not only was proclaimed in *words*, but also was demonstrated and attested to by *signs* and *wonders*. It was *seen* as well as heard. This is certainly evident in the public ministry of Jesus. It was characteristic as well of the ministries of the apostles and other early believers. Consider Philip of Samaria, for example.

> *Then Philip went down to the city of Samaria and preached Christ to them. And the multitudes with one accord heeded the things spoken by Philip, hearing and seeing the miracles which he did. For unclean spirits, crying with a loud voice, came out of many who were possessed; and many who were paralyzed and lame were healed. And there was great joy in that city.*[6]

When Jesus is proclaimed with power in a city, healing will come, deliverance will come, and joy will come. In the face of the presence of the Spirit's anointing, demons will manifest and be expelled. Deliverance will occur whenever Christ is preached in truth and power. If it is *not* happening, perhaps we need to take our spiritual pulse to see whether or not we are *truly* preaching Christ.

In our own day, billions of people live broken, hurting, and depressed lives without Christ. The need to preach Christ under the anointing of the Spirit is greater today than even in the time of Philip of Samaria. When Philip preached, people listened to his words, saw the miracles he performed, and responded in faith. The gospel of the Kingdom is something that people have to see as well as hear. We have gotten too expert in simply *preaching* the gospel—talking a good talk. There's more to proclaiming the gospel than that. Only the Church can name the name of Jesus and see blind eyes opened and the crippled walk. So it's not just how well we talk, but how well we learn to walk in the anointing that breaks the yoke. Miracles happened when Philip preached. When we preach Christ, we too should expect things to happen, because Jesus is the same yesterday, today, and forever, and because God is faithful. He wants to give us miracles every day.

One morning during a crusade in Pakistan, I saw a woman who had been born blind. She was sitting beside a sewer, and her eyes were all flat inside. Apparently, she had no eyeballs at all. I took a picture of her, because she represented to me all those people who sit in darkness without the light of the gospel. That night I proclaimed the name of Jesus, and said at the end of my sermon, "Holy Spirit, show this people that Jesus is the Son of God, that He was raised from the dead, and that He's the Savior!"

As I was in that realm in the Spirit, I heard a commotion. Looking around, I saw this same woman walking up onto the stage by herself. She came over to me and, speaking through our interpreter, said, "You know me. I was born blind. I've been blind for 60 years, but as this man [meaning me] was praying I saw flecks of light, and now I can see!" God had planted new eyes right there, and that woman could see for the first time in her life! I've seen God do this kind of thing over and over. Make no mistake about it, Jesus keeps His Word!

The Church has the anointing of God to set people and cities and nations free, but like Elijah when he was running from Jezebel, we are "hiding in the cave." Just as the Lord confronted Elijah in the cave, He asks us also, "What are you doing here? The people are broken and hurting." He who anointed and commissioned us, wants us to take His Word, His love, His compassion, His grace, and His mercy to the nations. "As the Father has sent Me, I also send you."

Field-Tested Keys to Releasing the Healing Anointing

OVER THE YEARS OF MY MINISTRY all around the world, I have learned some key principles about developing healing ministries, how to be sensitive to the Holy Spirit, and how to move in the realm of signs and wonders. These principles were not developed through cozy Bible studies in an ivory tower, but forged on the anvil of experience in the field.

These are living principles that I know work, because they exalt Jesus Christ.

Our ministry has taken us across Africa, from Zaire to Zambia, South Africa to the Ivory Coast, and from Cameroon to Nigeria. We have ministered across Eastern Europe, in the Czech Republic, Yugoslavia, and Hungary. We have also been to Russia, Switzerland, France, England, Germany, Holland, in Egypt, Israel, Taiwan, Japan, Korea, Pakistan, Malaysia, Central America, and Haiti, in the Caribbean. We have ministered from one side of the United States to the other. I have had the opportunity to lay hands on literally hundreds of thousands of people. Through all of this, I have discovered that these key principles work consistently, time after time. I want to share them with you to encourage you in seeking to walk in the healing anointing in your own life and ministry, touching those in need around you.

Key #1: Focus on the Finished Work of Christ

THIS FIRST KEY goes all the way back to Chapter Two. As I said then, preaching Christ and Him crucified is fundamental to the gospel. In fact, it *is* the gospel. There is no other gospel. Remember Paul's words,

And I, brethren, when I came to you, did not come with excellence of speech or of wisdom declaring to you the testimony of God. For I determined not to know anything among you except Jesus Christ and Him crucified. I was with you in weakness, in fear, and in much trembling. And my speech and my preaching were not with persuasive words of human wisdom, but in demonstration of the Spirit and of power, that your faith should not be in the wisdom of men but in the power of God. [7]

Even though Paul was a brilliant speaker, he realized his strength did not lie in brilliant speech, or even in carefully articulated arguments. I believe that one of the big problems in the Church over the last few centuries is that we have placed so much importance on good oratory, and so little on the power behind it. Let me put it this way: Whom would you rather follow? Someone who could present a brilliant six-week course on the theories and theology of resurrection, or someone who had actually *raised* the dead?

We have so emphasized learning, knowledge, and the excellency of human speech and human wisdom, that too often we neglect the anointing and the truly spiritual aspect of our lives. There's nothing wrong with knowledge and learning, but we need to keep them in perspective and keep our priorities in line. We must be careful to place primary importance on those things that are most important to the Lord.

The most important thing is to focus on the finished work of Jesus. That's what Paul meant when he said, "I determined not to know anything among you except Jesus Christ and Him crucified." Just before Jesus died, He cried out, "It is finished!"[8] The basic Greek word for "finished" is *tetelestia*, which means to do something perfectly perfect, or completely complete. Nothing more needs to be done for the salvation of humanity. Everything necessary to take away the pain and sickness of the world has been accomplished. Jesus completed it on the cross.

A divinely ordained exchange took place on Calvary, wherein Jesus took our sins and iniquities upon Himself, and healed us by His stripes. He became poor that we might become rich in God. He was punished so that we could be forgiven and have the peace of God. He took our shame, that we might have His glory. He was wounded so we could be healed. He suffered so that we could be made the righteousness of God. He took our curse that we might be blessed. He took our poverty that we might have abundance. He took our rejection that we might be accepted before God.[9]

As I focused on the finished work of Christ, as Paul did, I found that miracle after miracle started happening in my ministry. Focus on the finished work of Christ—the cross—and the saving, healing, and delivering power of God will be released.

Key #2: Proclaim the Word of God

THE SECOND KEY TO RELEASING THE HEALING ANOINTING is to proclaim the Word of God faithfully and without compromise. If we want to see the Spirit of God working in and through our lives, we must rely on the Word of God. It is vitally important that we take advantage of every opportunity we have to get the Word of God and the gospel of Christ before people.

Over the many years of my international ministry, I have been interviewed countless times on television and radio, and I have learned to make every moment count. One time in Zaire, I was interviewed on national television and radio. Because of difficulties in communication, I did not understand whether I had two minutes, twenty minutes, or an hour. In the first two minutes of the broadcast, the interviewer said to me, "Please tell us your name and where you come from."

I responded this way: "I've come to proclaim Jesus Christ and Him crucified on Calvary. Jesus took our sins and our sicknesses, and by His stripes we were healed. My name is Mahesh Chavda, and I come from the United States." I've learned to use any gap of time on the air to give the Word of God and focus on the cross and what Jesus did there.

Often, I'll ignore the specific questions because I want to focus on the immediate needs of the listeners. I'll proclaim God's Word, and explain that when people who are in distress cry out to Him, He will save them and heal them through Jesus Christ, His Son. Whenever we proclaim the Word of God in sincerity and truth, the Lord will be present to confirm His Word with signs and wonders. This is because, as the writer of Hebrews says, "For the word of God is living and powerful, and sharper than any two-edged sword, piercing even to the division of soul and spirit, and of joints and marrow, and is a discerner of the thoughts and intents of the heart."[10]

The apostle Paul wrote, "So then faith comes by hearing, and hearing by the word of God."[11] Jesus said, "If you have faith as a mustard seed, you will say to this mountain, 'Move from here to there,' and it will move; and nothing will be impossible for you."[12] How does faith come? It comes by hearing the Word of God. The Spirit of God takes the living Word of God and plants it in the hearts of hearers, where it gives birth to faith. *There is no substitute for proclaiming the Word of God.*

Key #3: Plead the Blood of Jesus

ANOTHER KEY TO RELEASING THE HEALING ANOINTING in our lives and ministries is to learn to recognize the power of pleading the blood of

Jesus. The Bible says in Revelation, "And they overcame him [satan] by the blood of the Lamb and by the word of their testimony..."[13] We are constantly doing battle with spiritual forces of darkness who oppose us with weapons that are not of flesh and blood. Alone, none of us can stand against the devil. We are not alone, however. As believers, we have been equipped by God with two weapons against which satan cannot stand: the Word of God, which includes the testimony of our saving faith in Christ *through* His Word, and the blood of Christ, as revealed in His finished work on the cross.

Sometimes we find the devil attacking our home, getting a foothold in our family situation. We start arguing back and forth and fighting and getting angry over little things. It's so easy to fall into the flesh. Other times, satan gets his hand into the Church, and congregations start gossiping and taking sides against each other on issues that are usually of little real importance. One of satan's central strategies is "divide and conquer," and he uses it with devastating effectiveness.

The way to experience victory over demonic attack at home and in the church is not by using human reasoning, arguments, or debates, but by using the weapons God has given us: His Word and the shed blood of Jesus. When we advance with this armament deployed, satan will flee. He cannot stand against the power of Jesus' blood. The old gospel hymn writers were right on target:

> *Would you be free from the burden of sin?*
> *There's pow'r in the blood, power in the blood;*
> *Would you o'er evil a victory win?*
> *There's wonderful pow'r in the blood.*
> *There is pow'r, pow'r,*
> *Wonder-working pow'r*
> *In the blood of the Lamb;*
> *There is pow'r, pow'r,*
> *Wonder-working pow'r*
> *In the precious blood of the Lamb.*[14]
>
> *What can wash away my sin?*
> *Nothing but the blood of Jesus;*

111

The Hidden Power of the Believer's Touch

What can make me whole again?
Nothing but the blood of Jesus.
This is all my hope and peace,
Nothing but the blood of Jesus;
This is all my righteousness,
Nothing but the blood of Jesus.
Oh! Precious is the flow
That makes me white as snow;
No other fount I know,
Nothing but the blood of Jesus.[15]

One of the hidden keys to releasing the healing through the believer's touch is the power released through the elements of communion. At critical seasons in my life, the Holy Spirit would impress me to take communion more often, on occasion even daily. I would either receive it before ministering to others, or I would take the elements with me and share them with those in need of healing. Through the elements of communion, we are often able to dynamically focus on the finished work of Christ on Calvary.

Who Himself bore our sins in His own body on the tree...by whose stripes you were healed.[16]

And when they had come to the place called Calvary, there they crucified Him.[17]

The sinless, spotless Son of God underwent the most horrendous and painful death on the cross. He is the Passover lamb who gave Himself for you and me. In the bread and the cup we meet this Passover lamb.

We discover that when the children of Israel were bitten by poisonous snakes and were dying, the Lord instructed Moses to make a bronze serpent and lift it up on a pole. Whoever looked upon it would be healed and live.[18] This was a shadow of Christ's redeeming work on Calvary. John 3:14 says, "And as Moses lifted up the serpent in the wilderness, even so must the Son of Man be lifted up."

Through the elements of communion we are looking afresh at the Lamb of God, partaking of the glory of Calvary, and "By His stripes, we are healed." I strongly believe that regular partaking of communion elements (some call it the Lord's Supper) will help facilitate and make effective the healing power of the believer's touch in our lives.

> *For I received from the Lord that which I also delivered to you: that the Lord Jesus on the same night in which He was betrayed took bread; and when He had given thanks, He broke it and said, "Take, eat; this is My body which is broken for you; do this in remembrance of Me." In the same manner He also took the cup after supper, saying, "This cup is the new covenant in My blood. This do, as often as you drink it, in remembrance of Me." For as often as you eat this bread and drink this cup, you proclaim the Lord's death till He comes.*[19]

Key #4: Invoke the Name of Jesus

THE FOURTH KEY TO RELEASING THE HEALING ANOINTING is to invoke the name of Jesus. I'm certainly not talking about some weird occultic incantation here, but calling on the divine authority and power of Christ Himself. God has warned us in His Word not to take His name in vain, and there's a good reason for it. When we invoke, or call on, the name of Jesus, the entire resources of Heaven are at hand to help us. You will remember that in Mark chapter 16, Jesus commanded His disciples to preach the gospel to every creature. He went on to say that signs would follow those who believed: casting out demons, speaking in tongues, taking up serpents and drinking poison with no ill effects, and healing the sick with a touch of the hand. All of these things, Jesus said, would be done *in His name*. There is power in the name of Jesus.

Once, when I was in the Ivory Coast doing a big crusade, a high government official asked for a few moments of my time. He came with his family, and the grandmother chose to be the spokesperson. Showing me a picture of their granddaughter, she said, "This is Angela. We sent her to Paris, France, to go to the university. She's quite bright, but after she got there, she fell in with some bad people, started taking cocaine, and is now a drug addict. She disappeared into the criminal underworld in Paris, and we have not heard one word from her for two years. The police can't find her. We have even sent private detectives to look for her, but she seems to be completely lost." Then the grandmother started crying; the mother and father started crying; the whole family started crying.

"Stop!" I said. "This is not a time to cry; this is a time to fight! Give me that picture. We're going to lay hands on this picture." After we had done so, I said, "Satan, this young lady does not belong to you. Her mother and father are believers in Jesus, and her grandmother is a believer in Jesus. In the name of Jesus Christ, take your hands off this girl! Angels of God, rescue this daughter! I send you now to bring her back to her family!"

I saw them again the next day; they were smiling and laughing. They told me that *four hours* after we prayed, Angela had called from Paris, crying, and said, "I don't know what happened, but I want to come home." That quickly, the veil had fallen from her eyes, and she was freed from her addiction. Why? There is power in the name of Jesus. When we speak His name, the resources of Heaven are loosed for us.

Key #5: Rely on the Mercy of God

THE HEALING ANOINTING CAN ALSO BE RELEASED when we learn to rely on the mercy of God. In Mark chapter 10, a blind man named Bartimaeus appealed to Jesus to heal him. Jesus had just left the city of Jericho, and Bartimaeus was sitting by the side of the road. As he heard Jesus approaching, he called out, "Jesus, Son of David, have mercy on me!"[20]

Although the surrounding crowd told Bartimaeus to be quiet, Jesus called the blind man forward. "So Jesus answered and said to him, 'What do you want Me to do for you?' The blind man said to Him, 'Rabboni, that I may receive my sight.' Then Jesus said to him, 'Go your way; your faith has made you well.' And immediately he received his sight and followed Jesus on the road."[21] Bartimaeus was healed and received his eyesight because he cried, "Lord, have mercy on me."

We can rely on the mercy of God. When we or those around us have a need, count on the mercy of God. We should not count on our rights as much as on the mercy of God. The Lord doesn't *owe* us anything, but He always responds to cries for mercy.

Your complete reliance on the compassionate and merciful heart of Jesus is more important than the words you speak. If you are plugged into the anointing of His Spirit, a few words or even one word may be sufficient.[22]

As a young pastor in 1974, I had already begun to see healings occur in my ministry in a major way. People were streaming in from many different places to receive prayer for healing. One family drove hundreds of miles from New Mexico to visit our church in Texas. A young father and mother had come with their five young children, two of whom were under two years of age. The other three were only a few years older. The mother had recently discovered that she had advanced breast cancer. The cancer had spread widely and had basically eaten her up.

I remember that as I laid hands on this woman to pray for her, I did not feel anything. At that time I had no faith, but I said, "Oh Lord, look on these little ones, and have mercy on this family." The next day this mother went for more tests at a hospital in a neighboring city. Not one single trace of cancer could be found anywhere in her body. All the malignancy had disappeared!

I believe that I was able to touch the heart of God by simply crying out, just like Bartimaeus, "Lord, have mercy! Lord have mercy!" *We can rely on the mercy of God.*

Setting the Atmosphere of the Healing Touch

YOU ARE AN EMISSARY of the Lord and His anointing. It is important, as you start touching people, to realize that Christ is the healer and not you. Yet the Bible says, "This treasure we hold in earthen vessels."[23] Walk therefore in the consciousness of the presence of Christ. He has said, "I will never leave you nor forsake you."[24] Know therefore in every situation that His presence and anointing are with you. Acknowledging His presence in every circumstance will change the atmosphere around you. In the midst of pain and grief, Jesus is still the King of Glory. His authority, love, and compassion remain unchanged. You must remain plugged in to this heavenly reality in every circumstance. In this manner you will be able to bring Christ's answer and His provision into your circumstance. This is what I call the atmosphere of the glory of the Lord.

Isaiah chapter 6 holds some profound truths. Verse 1 says, "In the year that King Uzziah died, I saw the Lord sitting on a throne, high and lifted up, and the train of His robe filled the temple." King Uzziah died with leprosy. In the midst of these circumstances, Isaiah plugged into the glory and presence of God. To be an emissary of the believer's touch, we must grow in the anointing and be plugged into the heavenly presence which is the glory of the Lord. In the midst of great pain in my life during the time of Aaron's birth, as I stood before thousands of Africans in the city of Kinshasa in the Congo, the atmosphere suddenly changed, and I sensed the presence of His glory. It is in this atmosphere that nothing is impossible with our God.

You will not become an expert overnight in ministering the touch of healing. But as you are open to be used to minister this healing touch, this consciousness of His presence will start to grow. You may not see cancers fall away the first day you touch someone, but my prayer and my instruction is to keep persevering. The Scriptures say, "We go from glory to glory."[25] This is what will happen in your life as you are faithful.

The Scripture also tells us that if we are faithful in little, God will give us more.[26] Be excited any time there is a change for the better when you touch someone in the name of Christ. I have learned to aggressively thank and praise God for any improvement, any miracle. This seems to set a pathway for healing. God is pleased when we are faithful—full of faith. Once you start touching people, stay in this path. Don't allow temporary setbacks to discourage you. I have learned that the healing touch is more an art than a science. Your persistence will accrue rich dividends.

You will remember from Chapter Five how Elijah seemed to have set up several roadblocks to his disciple, Elisha. At several junctures he told Elisha to stop following him. Elijah kept saying, "Stay here; I have to go on." This was not disobedience, but desperation. Elisha passed the test, insisting again and again, "I will not leave you." Eventually he got the payoff. He received a double portion of the miracle mantle of Elijah, the great servant of God. Remember also that Elisha let this mantle permeate his entire being so much so that when he died, his very bones were saturated with this healing virtue. In Second Kings 13:21, a person who had just died was raised to life again after accidentally touching Elisha's bones. Even the bones of Elisha could raise someone from the coils of death! This is the God that we serve and the kind of anointing that can flow through us, that can make the believer's touch so powerful. I would encourage all who desire the believer's touch to seek every opportunity to soak in the "mantle of Elijah"—the presence of the Holy Spirit. Find opportunities to have believers lay hands on you who themselves flow in the anointing, and stir up the gifts in your life.

As you flow in this atmosphere, the Holy Spirit may bring to your attention areas in your life that hinder you from flowing in this anointing. Perhaps inordinate anger hinders you. Perhaps it could be self-pity and self-love. It could be an unclean habit. Be willing to bring it to the Lord with repentance and prayer. Get released from these hindrances. The key we find that was so apparent in the ministry of our Lord Jesus Christ is the unhindered flow of the healing anointing that He had—always with a heart full of humility and compassion. Any sense of pride will deflate the strength of the anointing. Know that when there is a healing, it's always Christ who gets the glory. The more aggressively you give Him praise and glory the more you will steward the healing mantle in your life.

This mantle of healing will joyfully restore us as we extend a heart of compassion and mercy to all those around us who are in some kind of need, especially the poor. Jesus said, "He has anointed me to preach the gospel to the poor."[27] A lack of compassion towards the poor will create a block to the anointing. In addition, I have found that racism, anti-Semitism and bigotry cannot dwell in a vessel that carries the anointing. When I see need around me, I get stirred to sow a seed to help answer that need. Sowing a seed will fertilize your vision for releasing the healing touch.

When I began to see that when I laid hands on people, sickness withdrew, and pain disappeared, and when the blind started seeing and the cancers evaporated, I was excited. I knew I could not do it, but it was the virtue of this awesome King of Glory, Jesus Christ of Nazareth. With this excitement came a passion to exalt Christ and make a difference through the laying on of hands. I learned that there could be setbacks from time to time, but the Lord's truth never changes. I learned in some circumstances to pray for a situation and pray again and again. As you extend the believer's touch, know that in some circumstances you may have to lay on hands every day. Sometimes the healing may be instant, and certain times you may have to lay on hands many times.

I have often been asked, "Pastor, may we pray more than once for a situation?" I tell them, "Pray and pray again." You find in Second Kings 13:18,19 that Elisha instructs the king to strike the ground with the arrows. The striking of the arrows was symbolic of prophetic prayer. The king struck only three times and stopped and Elisha, the man with the mantle, became angry and told him he should have struck several more times for the circumstances to change completely. We find this even in the life of Jesus when He lays on hands more than once. In Mark 8:22-25 a blind man was brought to Him. Jesus spat on his eyes and laid hands on him and asked if he saw anything. The man replied, "I see men like trees walking." Then Jesus once again put His hands on his eyes and the blind man was restored completely. Notice that Jesus did not rebuke this man for lacking faith after He had prayed the first time. I feel that this is a model that the Lord left for us to encourage us to pray through. During the initial days of my ministry a shadowy presence would come and whisper, "What if this person is not healed? What if in this terminal situation this person dies?" I learned over the years to do as Isaiah did—to keep my eyes looking heavenward and see the Lord. It is the Lord who is the healer, and He changes not. I learned that God is sovereign and that He is Lord and King. He can certainly take someone home any time He wishes. As for me, I have received a commission from Him, "Go into all the world...preach the gospel...these signs will follow those who believe...they will lay hands on the sick, and they will recover." I have chosen to obey the Great Commission.

Whether it is healing the sick or delivering the demonized, touching people for the Lord means learning how to release the anointing, to unleash the rivers of living water within us in order to break the enemy's grip on the hearts, souls, and bodies of the lost and needy everywhere.

This involves not only breaking the power of sickness, but also breaking the power of generational curses. Jesus came to destroy the works of the devil. None of the dams or other obstructions that satan has erected on earth or in the lives of people can withstand the flood of the healing river of God as it washes over the land. *Life grows where the river flows!*

Endnotes

1. Mt. 28:18b-19.

2. Mk. 16:15b,17.

3. Jn. 20:19-22.

4. Mk. 1:14-15,21-22.

5. Mk. 1:23-28.

6. Acts 8:5-8.

7. 1 Cor. 2:1-5.

8. Jn. 19:30b.

9. Consider these Scriptures that show us what Christ's death on the cross accomplishes for us: Healing (Isa. 53:4-5; 1 Pet. 2:24; Mt. 8:17); Abundance (2 Cor. 8:9; Deut. 28:47; 2 Cor. 9:8); Forgiveness and peace (Isa 53:5); Blessing, and breaking the curse (Gal. 3:13-14; Deut. 28:2-13); Righteousness (2 Cor. 5:21; Isa. 53:11); Acceptance (Ps. 88:3-6; Eph. 1:6; Mt. 27:46); Glory (Heb. 2:10).

10. Heb. 4:12.

11. Rom. 10:17.

12. Mt. 17:20b.

13. Rev. 12:11a.

14. Lewis E. Jones, "There Is Power in the Blood," public domain.

15. Robert Lowry, "Nothing but the Blood," public domain.

16. 1 Pet. 2:24.

17. Lk. 23:33a.

18. Num. 21:9
19. 1 Cor. 11:23-26
20. Mk. 10:47b.
21. Mk. 10:51-52.
22. See Mark 5:41.
23. 2 Cor. 4:7.
24. Heb. 13:5.
25. 2 Cor. 3:18.
26. Mt. 25:21.
27. Lk. 4:18.

Chapter Eight

Breaking the Enemy's Grip

IN CHAPTER FOUR I RELATED THE STORY of how the Lord raised a young boy named Katshinyi from the dead during a crusade I was conducting in Zaire. The year after that crusade, I returned to that same area for another series of meetings. When I landed at the airport at Kinshasa, the Lord spoke to me and said, "I want you to baptize these people."

At first, this posed a problem for me. I am an evangelical Christian who was originally ordained as a Baptist minister, so I thought, *Where can I find a large enough water tank?* I fully anticipated that thousands of people would come to the Lord, and I felt that this time I was supposed to give them the full package of "repent, be baptized, and receive the Holy Spirit." Indeed, there were thousands of people in animism or witchcraft religions who converted to the Lord. Where could I baptize so many? Then I realized that the Congo River runs alongside the city of Kinshasa. So, I held a baptism service on the banks of the river.

The Congo River Claimed My Shoes

IN THAT PART OF THE COUNTRY the Congo River serves as the border between Zaire to the east and the nation of the Congo to the west. Directly across the river from Kinshasa was the city of Brazzaville, which was in the Congo. Because there were frequent exchanges of gunfire across the river on both sides, no one could hold a meeting at the river's edge without government permission.

One of the people whom I had led to the Lord in my services was a general in the Zairian army. I asked him to help me get permission for the baptism service. He told me that he could arrange it for me, but that I would have to take some of his soldiers with me. I told him that I didn't need any soldiers for the service, and thought that the people might be frightened by their presence. The general was adamant, however. He insisted that soldiers be present.

I reluctantly agreed. It was a strange feeling to descend the hill to the riverbank accompanied by soldiers armed with automatic weapons. Several thousand people gathered at the water's edge, including approximately one hundred local pastors who were present to assist me in conducting the baptisms. Since I was the leader, all the African pastors looked to me to be the first to step into the river.

I hadn't originally planned to, but, with all eyes on me, I realized that I had better go in. I was wearing brand-new Nike® jogging shoes that I had purchased specifically for this trip to Africa. As soon as I stepped into the water, the river began to suck at my feet. Thick mud and centuries of gunk had gathered on the river bottom. The more I tried to get farther into the water, the more the current and the gunk pulled at my feet. It was a tremendous challenge just pulling my legs up. That river was so gunky that it sucked up my shoes. I was able to get my feet loose, but the Congo River claimed my shoes.

Suddenly, the Log Opened Its Mouth

FINALLY, I GOT TO A PLACE IN THE RIVER where the water was up to my waist. My legs had sunk halfway to my knees in the mud and gunk of the river bottom. I could move sideways, but not forward. I was about to speak to the people when suddenly the soldiers started firing their machine guns. At first, I thought they were firing at the people. As I turned around, I heard bullets whizzing by me and I realized that they were shooting in my direction. What had I done? Then I saw that they were shooting at two or three logs that were floating near me. What a time for target practice! Suddenly, one of those "logs" opened its mouth, and I realized they were *crocodiles*! The soldiers were shooting to drive the crocodiles away. I said, "Lord, You didn't tell me that I would have to go into a river infested with crocodiles!"

The Mad Woman Thought We Were Swimming

WHEN ALL WAS READY, I indicated to my helpers to bring the people in. A couple of the African pastors were assisting me, and the others were spread out over about a hundred yards or so along the riverbank. We baptized more than three thousand people that day. It was a glorious time!

The climax of the day, however, was when the mad woman joined us. She had on a tee shirt that went halfway to her knees, and had been living in the bush like an animal for years. In that land where many people are deep into witchcraft religions, sometimes they lose their faculties. Many people had heard this woman crying out in the wilderness like an animal. From time to time some of them threw her some food.

As this poor woman watched from the top of the hill as we dunked thousands of people in the river, in her crazy mind she thought that we were swimming. She ran down the hill screaming at the people in the water, "I want to swim, too! Let me swim!" She was at the other end of the crowd from me, so there was little I could do. She kept screaming and starting running through the crowd, attacking and biting people.

Finally, a group of the pastors at that end got together and, without consulting me, said to her, "Come on in. We'll let you swim." Two of the ushers helped her into the water. Then, a couple of the pastors took her by the arms and dunked her, saying, "We baptize you in the name of Jesus Christ." When they brought her up out of the water, she was in her right mind, restored, and completely healed!

What a glorious and awesome day that was! We baptized over three thousand people; I shared the river with crocodiles; I gave up my Nike® jogging shoes as an offering to the Congo River; and a woman beloved of God was released from the bondage of madness and demonic oppression into the freedom and light of Christ!

There Are Three Ways That God Meets the Needs of Humanity

THIS BAPTISMAL SERVICE IN THE CONGO RIVER helps illustrate the three different ways that God meets the needs of humanity. First, He saves us from sin. The three thousand Africans we baptized that day were giving testimony to how their sins had been forgiven and they had found new life in Christ. Secondly, God heals our diseases. Many of those who were baptized had also been divinely healed from some kind of sickness or injury. Thirdly, the Lord delivers us from demonic oppression. Again, many of those in the baptismal crowd had been released from demonic spirits which had possessed and bound them. This was particularly true of the mad woman who wanted to swim with us.

We find this threefold redemption expressed in Psalm 107: "Then they cried out to the Lord in their trouble, and He saved them out of their distresses. He sent His word and healed them, and delivered them from their destructions."[1] With His Word the Lord saves us from our "distresses," heals us, and delivers us from our "destructions."

In Exodus 15:26b God says, "I am the Lord who heals you." This phrase translates one of the seven redemption or covenant names of God, *Jehovah-Rapha*. Whenever God reveals one of His names in Scripture, He reveals an aspect of His nature and character. God is a healer by *nature*. He cannot get away from it; it is part of who He is.

The blessing of the name *Jehovah-Rapha* was secured for us through the atoning work of Christ on Calvary. We are saved, healed, and delivered by the "Word" of God who became flesh and dwelled among us. As I have already said, the work of Jesus is finished. It is complete, it is glorious, and it can stand up against any kind of argument. In a way we can never fully understand, Jesus took our sin, our pain, and our sickness. Every tear, every pain, every grief, every sorrow—Jesus knows them all. It is supernatural, and we don't have to analyze it as much as receive and experience it by faith.

Isaiah the prophet wrote, "Surely He has borne our griefs and carried our sorrows; yet we esteemed Him stricken, smitten by God, and afflicted. But He was wounded for our transgressions, He was bruised for our iniquities; the chastisement for our peace was upon Him, and by His stripes we are healed."[2] Referring to these verses, Simon Peter wrote of Jesus, "who Himself bore our sins in His own body on the tree, that we, having died to sins, might live for righteousness—by whose stripes you were healed."[3] All healing and miracles are based on the atoning work of Jesus, and since "Jesus Christ is the same yesterday, today, and forever,"[4] what He did two thousand years ago, He still does today. What He made available to the people of ancient Palestine, He makes available to us.

I have seen people born blind receive their sight, cripples walk, and even seen a dead person raised to life. Divine healing *is* for us *today*. God wants to release an army of anointed workers who will bring the healing anointing to the nations. Often, however, we will have to assist in breaking the barriers that hinder people from receiving healing.

Common Barriers to Healing

I HAVE BEEN ACTIVELY INVOLVED in healing ministry for over 25 years; and in my experience, I have learned that there are many different factors that can come into play making it difficult for a person to receive healing. It's not that the Lord doesn't want to heal, but that the person seeking healing is not, for some reason, in the spiritual *place* for healing. Remember the story of Gary from Chapter Four, who couldn't receive his healing until he recognized Christ's *unconditional* lordship over his life.

Whenever we encounter difficulty in healing, whether for ourselves or for someone we are praying for, it would be helpful to examine the situation and ask the Lord for insight regarding the presence of a hindrance. Out of my years of experience, I have identified 15 common barriers to healing.

1. *Ignorance of the Word of God.* Remember, "faith comes by hearing, and hearing by the word of God."[5] "Therefore My people have gone into captivity, because they have no knowledge..."[6] Knowledge of God's Word builds faith, including faith in Him as a healer. Ignorance of His Word inhibits faith.

2. *Unbelief.* This ties in with number one. Unbelief is sin. It is evil and will prevent someone from coming into God's promises. "Now He could do no mighty work there, except that He

laid His hands on a few sick people and healed them. And He marveled because of their unbelief."[7] "Beware, brethren, lest there be in any of you an evil heart of unbelief in departing from the living God; but exhort one another daily, while it is called 'Today,' lest any of you be hardened through the deceitfulness of sin."[8]

3. *Unforgiveness*. Holding onto bitterness and anger will hinder someone from receiving the healing power of God. One must *decide* to forgive; the emotion will follow. "And whenever you stand praying, if you have anything against anyone, forgive him, that your Father in heaven may also forgive you your trespasses. But if you do not forgive, neither will your Father in heaven forgive your trespasses."[9]

4. *Lethargy*. Apprehending a healing may require diligently seeking God's face. "But without faith it is impossible to please Him, for he who comes to God must believe that He is, and that He is a rewarder of those who diligently seek Him."[10] "O God, You are my God; early will I seek You; my soul thirsts for You; my flesh longs for You in a dry and thirsty land where there is no water."[11] "For I will pour water on him who is thirsty, and floods on the dry ground; I will pour My Spirit on your descendants, and My blessing on your offspring."[12]

5. *Pride*. God gives grace to the humble but resists the proud. This, too, involves a *personal* decision. "But He gives more grace. Therefore He says: 'God resists the proud, but gives grace to the humble.'"[13] "For thus says the High and Lofty One who inhabits eternity, whose name is Holy: 'I dwell in the high and holy place, with him who has a contrite and humble spirit, to revive the spirit of the humble, and to revive the heart of the contrite ones.'"[14]

6. *Lack of persistence*. This is related to but not identical with lethargy. We should never give up in our pursuit of healing, unless the Lord tells us, as He told Paul, "My grace is sufficient for you, for My strength is made perfect in weakness."[15] "Ask,

and it will be given to you; seek, and you will find; knock, and it will be opened to you. For everyone who asks receives, and he who seeks finds, and to him who knocks it will be opened."[16]

7. *Unconfessed sin.* "When I kept silent, my bones grew old through my groaning all the day long. For day and night Your hand was heavy upon me; my vitality was turned into the drought of summer. I acknowledged my sin to You, and my iniquity I have not hidden. I said, 'I will confess my transgressions to the Lord,' and You forgave the iniquity of my sin."[17]

8. *Neglect of the poor.* "Is this not the fast that I have chosen: to loose the bonds of wickedness, to undo the heavy burdens, to let the oppressed go free, and that you break every yoke? Is it not to share your bread with the hungry, and that you bring to your house the poor who are cast out; when you see the naked, that you cover him, and not hide yourself from your own flesh? Then your light shall break forth like the morning, your healing shall spring forth speedily, and your righteousness shall go before you; the glory of the Lord shall be your rear guard."[18]

9. *Rejection of the Holy Spirit.* Traditions of men keep some from receiving the agent of healing, the Holy Spirit. The anointing breaks the yoke. "It shall come to pass in that day that his burden will be taken away from your shoulder, and his yoke from your neck, and the yoke will be destroyed because of the anointing oil."[19]

10. *History of involvement with the occult or false religions.* *Every* connection must be cut. "You shall not bow down to their gods, nor serve them, nor do according to their works; but you shall utterly overthrow them and completely break down their sacred pillars. So you shall serve the Lord your God, and He will bless your bread and your water. And I will take sickness away from the midst of you. No one shall suffer miscarriage or be barren in your land; I will fulfill the number of your days."[20]

11. *The presence of evil spirits.* Demons can cause physical or emotional sickness. "And behold, there was a woman who had

a spirit of infirmity eighteen years, and was bent over and could in no way raise herself up. But when Jesus saw her, He called her to Him and said to her, 'Woman, you are loosed from your infirmity.' And He laid His hands on her, and immediately she was made straight, and glorified God."[21]

12. *Negative confessions*. What we say about ourselves or others is important and can affect us, either in hindering or helping the healing process. We must renounce all negative talk. "If you confess with your mouth the Lord Jesus and believe in your heart that God has raised Him from the dead, you will be saved."[22] "Finally, brethren, whatever things are true, whatever things are noble, whatever things are just, whatever things are pure, whatever things are lovely, whatever things are of good report, if there is any virtue and if there is anything praiseworthy—meditate on these things."[23]

13. *Wanting to see before believing*. Jesus said, "Did I not say to you that if you would believe you would see the glory of God?"[24] The law of the Spirit requires belief first, then seeing. "Jesus said to him, 'Thomas, because you have seen Me, you have believed. Blessed are those who have not seen and yet have believed.' "[25]

14. *The presence of a family curse*. The curse can be broken on the basis of the atonement of Christ. "Christ has redeemed us from the curse of the law, having become a curse for us (for it is written, 'Cursed is everyone who hangs on a tree'), that the blessing of Abraham might come upon the Gentiles in Christ Jesus, that we might receive the promise of the Spirit through faith."[26]

15. *Anti-Semitism*. The Jews are the chosen people of God and still have a central role in His plan and purpose for humanity. Throughout Scripture, those nations and peoples who sought to destroy Israel brought curses and destruction upon themselves. Even the nations that God used to bring judgment on the people of Israel for their sins were in turn judged by God for their own wickedness. We need to pray for the Jews and for the

nation of Israel. "Pray for the peace of Jerusalem: 'May they prosper who love you. Peace be within your walls, prosperity within your palaces.'"[27]

Curses Hinder Healing

WHILE IT IS CERTAINLY TRUE that most physical sickness has a physiological basis, it is equally true that much of it has a spiritual basis. As I mentioned above, both the presence of evil spirits and a history of involvement with the occult or with false religions can hinder healing. As I have prayed for literally hundreds of thousands of people around the world, I have discovered that demonic oppression is real and that curses are real.

When I first started praying for people years ago, I felt the Lord saying to me time after time, "Break the curse, break the curse." Even though I didn't fully understand what it meant at the time, I began to pray, "In Jesus' name, I break the curse." Immediately I saw some amazing results in my ministry.

I remember a woman in Michigan who had a severe form of diabetes, and after I prayed to break the curse, she was totally set free. Her doctor told her she did not need insulin anymore.

I kept on praying with people to break the curse, and the Lord said to me one day, "Do you know what you're doing?" I didn't really know, so the Lord started revealing to me what curses are, how they come, and how we can break them. I discovered that the Bible has a lot to say about curses, mentioning them over two hundred times.

For example, it says in Proverbs, "Like a flitting sparrow, like a flying swallow, so a curse without cause shall not alight."[28] There are causes for curses, however. Deuteronomy 27:15-26 pronounces curses on these activities: idolatry, contempt for parents, stealing a neighbor's property, leading a blind person astray, perversion of justice, sexual immorality and perversion, attacking one's neighbor secretly, accepting money to kill an innocent person, and rejection of and disobedience to God's law.

In these and other ways, people and even nations can open themselves up to a curse. In Genesis chapter 12, God pronounced a special blessing on the descendants of Abraham. Consequently, anyone who tried to curse the nation of Israel brought a curse upon himself instead.

The Bible also makes clear that curses are not restricted to only one generation. "The Lord is longsuffering and abundant in mercy, forgiving iniquity and transgression; but He by no means clears the guilty, visiting the iniquity of the fathers on the children to the third and fourth generation."[29] I have found at times that as I pray for people, the Lord gives me a word of knowledge and leads me to say to them, "Your father was a member of a secret society, wasn't he?" Many people, even Christians, join these secret groups, yoking themselves to unbelievers, and often unwittingly, speak all kinds of evil oaths upon themselves and their families, opening the door for curses to take hold.

If we're not careful, we can speak curses upon ourselves. I prayed once for a young woman who was very sensitive about her appearance. Because she did not like the way her thighs looked she said, "I hate these thighs," and unknowingly placed a curse on herself. She started getting sick, suffering all kinds of different pains. When I prayed for her, I had her lay her hands on her legs and bless them, because, after all, like them or not, they took her places.

There is power in our words, especially if we're Christians. That is why it is so vitally important for all of us who are parents to speak blessings upon our children. I couldn't begin to count the number of young men and women I have prayed for who were fighting against the curse of hateful words from their parents, such as, "You'll never amount to anything." As believers, we need to make sure that we control our tongues and speak only life and blessing. Words have power, for good or for evil.

Recognize the Symptoms of a Generational Family Curse

SIMPLY STATED, the key to experiencing the blessings of God and avoiding His curses is to read, receive, and obey His Word. This choice is laid out plainly in Deuteronomy chapter 28. The first 14 verses describe the blessings that will come to individuals and to the nation if they pay heed to the Word of the Lord, while the remainder of the chapter lines out the curses that will follow from disobedience.

I have also found in my own experience that often there are Christians who are sincerely trying to serve and obey the Lord the best they can, yet are hindered by some kind of shadowy force that keeps them from getting the blessing of coming through into victory. Upon further insight or examination, the cause turns out to be a generational family curse. Over the years I have discovered some characteristic symptoms that may reveal the presence of such a curse:

1. *A family history of continuing mental and emotional breakdown.*

2. *A family history of repeated or chronic sicknesses that have no medical explanation.*

3. *A family history of continuing barrenness, miscarriages, or intense female problems.*

4. *A family history of marital problems, marriage breakdowns, and divorce.*

5. *A family history of continuing alienation between children and parents.*

6. *A family history of continuing financial insufficiency, even when income seems to be adequate.*

7. *A family history of a tendency to be accident-prone.*

8. *A family history of involvement in the occult or false religions.*

If a person is having difficulty receiving a healing, be sensitive to the possibility of the presence of a curse for one or more of these reasons. Questioning the person may yield the needed information. Also, be sensitive to the Lord's voice; He may give you a word of knowledge regarding the situation.

For example, some years ago I prayed for a woman who was eaten up with rheumatoid arthritis. Her fingers were curled and twisted, and she was experiencing tremendous pain. As I began to pray for her, I sensed the Holy Spirit directing me to ask, "What are you wearing around your neck?" It was hidden under her sweater. She showed me a silver necklace with a cross-like object hanging from it. Actually, it was an *ankh*, an ancient Egyptian fertility symbol that is now commonly used in satanic worship. This was a fine, committed Christian lady.

I asked her, "When did your arthritis start?"

She said, "It started suddenly two years ago last Christmas."

"When did you start wearing this necklace?"

"Two years ago last Christmas. My children gave it to me as a Christmas gift."

I told her to take it off. As I prayed, I led her to renounce the necklace, its occultic and pagan associations, and her involvement by wearing it. In a matter of moments her fingers straightened out, her pain went away, and she was completely healed.

Jesus Christ Can Break Every Curse

THE GOOD NEWS THAT WE CAN SHARE with every person we meet who is bound by sin or sickness or a family curse is that Jesus Christ can forgive every sin, heal every sickness, and break every curse. Each of us bears responsibility for our own actions before God, so we can't blame everything on satan. We are responsible for our own choices. At the same time, sin, sickness, and curses are very much the works of the devil, which he has wrought in our lives. Jesus brings us hope. John the apostle wrote, "He who sins is of the devil, for the devil has sinned from the beginning. For this purpose the Son of God was manifested, that He might destroy the works of the devil."[30]

Jesus came to "destroy the works of the devil," and He accomplished this by becoming sin for us and by being made a curse for us on the cross. Look again at Paul's statement in Galatians: "Christ has redeemed us from the curse of the law, having become a curse for us (for it is written, 'Cursed is everyone who hangs on a tree'), that the blessing of Abraham might come upon the Gentiles in Christ Jesus, that we might receive the promise of the Spirit through faith."[31]

The Bible says that every curse can be broken through Jesus Christ. His atoning work on the cross is the legal basis for removing curses.

132

Satan no longer has the authority to us or our children, because we stand on the Word of God and on the work of Christ. On Calvary, all the weight of every sin and all the consequences of every curse were laid on Jesus.

Jesus' finished work on the cross has totally satisfied every legal requirement for our deliverance. Through Christ, we have been delivered *legally*, or *positionally*, before God, but now God wants us to come *experientially* into His blessing. We already possess it by *faith*, according to His will and purpose; now He wants us to possess it by *experience*.

When God brought the nation of Israel into the Promised Land, He told them, "I have given you this land. Go in and possess it." Did He mean it? Of course, He did. The land was theirs; they already possessed it *legally* in God's purpose. Before they could possess it in actual *experience*, however, they had to go in and fight for every square inch of it. God gave them success over their enemies, but they had to go in and possess it.

In the same way, God now wants us to "go in" and possess the blessings. The Israelites entered Canaan under the leadership of Joshua, whose name means "Jehovah is salvation." The name *Jesus* is the Greek form of *Joshua*. As believers, led by our "Joshua," the Lord Jesus Christ, we enter the Promised Land of blessings and deliverance, provision and abundance, and victory.

Repent, Renounce, and Release

THE BASIS FOR HEALING AND DELIVERANCE is the Word of God. It's not emotions, and it's not experience, because these things can change. God's Word does not change. Jesus said, "Heaven and earth will pass away, but My words will by no means pass away."[32] Herein is established a clear scriptural basis upon which we can break every curse over every family.

We must confess any known sins, as well as any unknown sins that the Holy Spirit reveals to us, confess our faith in Jesus Christ, and commit ourselves to obey the Word of God to the best of our ability. We must renounce every work of and every connection with the occult, or with false religions. This involves recognizing the problem and then repenting on behalf of our ancestors and for the sake of our families: "Lord, we repent, and we renounce every contact with the powers of darkness." Coupled with this is the need to forgive anyone or any group who has harmed either us, our families, or our ancestors.

After repenting and renouncing, we then need to release ourselves in the name of Jesus Christ. This process of repenting, renouncing, and releasing is one of the living words that God has given me, through which I have seen thousands of people instantly receive miracles of healing and deliverance.

Once, while holding a crusade in Zambia, I felt the Lord direct me one night to pray to break the curse of barrenness. We were in the remote northwest part of the country, and there were six thousand people in attendance. I said, "The Lord wants me to break the curse of barrenness right now. Any married women who have never had children but who want them, come on up."

Around five hundred women came up. As I got ready to pray for them, I felt the Lord say, "Not yet. They have been involved in witchcraft. First, break the yoke of witchcraft." It seemed like a strange word, yet I have learned through much experience to trust and not question the Lord. So I asked the women, "How many of you have been to a witch doctor?" Almost all of them—497—responded that they had visited a witch doctor. Right then and there I led them to renounce the witchcraft and their involvement in it. Afterwards, I prayed to break the curse of barrenness.

In African culture, if a woman does not bear any children within three years, her husband can divorce her and send her home. So, these five hundred women were under a lot of social and cultural pressure.

I returned to the same area the following year. One of the sponsoring pastors from the previous year said to me, "Brother Mahesh, I don't know about the other women, but last year 29 barren women from my church came up for prayer. Today, every one of them is either pregnant or already has a new baby."

There is power in the Word of God. Christ has redeemed us from the curse; they are broken in His name through the power of His blood. He turns the brackish swamps of our hurting lives into the refreshing floods of God's blessings. *He turns bitter waters into sweet!*

Endnotes

1. Ps. 107:19-20.
2. Is. 53:4-5.
3. 1 Pet. 2:24.
4. Heb. 13:8.
5. Rom. 10:17.
6. Is. 5:13.
7. Mk. 6:5-6a.
8. Heb. 3:12-13.
9. Mk. 11:25-26.
10. Heb. 11:6.
11. Ps. 63:1.
12. Is. 44:3.
13. Jas. 4:6.
14. Is. 57:15.
15. 2 Cor. 12:9a.
16. Mt. 7:7-8.
17. Ps. 32:3-5.
18. Is. 58:6-8.
19. Is. 10:27.
20. Ex. 23:24-26.
21. Lk. 13:11-13.
22. Rom. 10:9.

23. Phil. 4:8.

24. Jn. 11:40.

25. Jn. 20:29.

26. Gal. 3:13-14.

27. Ps. 122:6-7.

28. Prov. 26:2.

29. Num. 14:18.

30. 1 Jn. 3:8.

31. Gal. 3:13-14.

32. Mt. 24:35.

Chapter Nine

Turning Bitter Water Into Sweet

EARLIER IN THIS BOOK I said that simple acts of faith release the miracles of God. In my ministry all around the world I have seen for myself over and over how true this is in practice. I couldn't begin to number the times I have seen the healing anointing of God released on an individual, and sometimes on a whole group of people, after a simple expression of faith on their part. We find this same principle active throughout the Bible. One good example is found in the life of the prophet Elisha.

> *Then the men of the city said to Elisha, "Please notice, the situation of this city is pleasant, as my lord sees; but the water is bad, and the ground barren." And he said, "Bring me a new bowl, and put salt in it." So they brought it to him. Then he went out to the source of the water, and cast in the salt there, and said, "Thus says the Lord: 'I have healed this water; from it there shall be no more death or barrenness.'" So the water remains healed to this day, according to the word of Elisha which he spoke.*[1]

The "city" of this passage is Jericho. The ground around the city was barren, probably due to the "bad" water. There was nothing special or magic about either the "new bowl" or the "salt" that Elisha called for;

they may have been symbolic of the beginning of a new day of the Lord's favor. The healing was in the Word of the Lord, not in the act of sprinkling salt into the water. By a simple act of faith and obedience on Elisha's part, the Lord healed the water. Notice that the healing was permanent; the water remained pure even to the day of the Scripture writer.

In fact, the water has remained pure for well over two thousand years. Once, when I was in Israel, I had the opportunity to drink from this spring near Jericho, and the water is still pure, sweet, and refreshing. By contrast, many of the other springs and water sources in that general region of the country are brackish.

Delivered by the Blood of the Lamb

IN HIS DESIRE TO BRING HUMANITY INTO REDEMPTION, God has always been in the business of turning bitter water into sweet. One of the most compelling biblical demonstrations of this is found in the record of God's dealings with the Israelites in the Book of Exodus.

After Joseph died, and all his brothers as well, along with that entire generation of Hebrews who had gone into Egypt, their descendants multiplied greatly. Eventually, they were enslaved by the Egyptians and spent four hundred years in bondage. During this time, many of them lived in sin, adopting the idolatrous religion and worship practices of their slave lords, the Egyptians. They suffered from all kinds of sicknesses. They worked as forced laborers in the stone quarries of Egypt and in building the great monuments of Pharaoh.

As a result, hundreds of them—perhaps thousands—had an arm or a leg crushed. There were many cripples, and many were weak or blinded by malnutrition, because as slaves they probably were not well fed. They lived in abject poverty. In their desperate plight they cried out to God, and He delivered them.

God sent Moses, through whom He performed great signs before Pharaoh as demonstrations of His power and sovereignty, and as judgment for Pharaoh's stubborn defiance. God turned the waters of the Nile to blood. He sent plagues of frogs, lice, flies, hail, and locusts that attacked animals, people, and produce. He sent diseases to kill livestock and boils and sores to afflict the Egyptians. He sent a three-day darkness over the land. In each of these, the Israelites were spared while the Egyptians suffered greatly.

Finally, in one incredible night, the Lord devastated Egypt and delivered His people. Through Moses, God commanded the Israelites to take a male yearling lamb, and on the 14th day of the month, slaughter it and spread its blood on the lintels and doorposts of their houses. They were to roast the lamb and eat it along with unleavened bread and bitter herbs. They were to eat "in haste," with their belts and sandals on and their staffs in their hands—ready to depart on a moment's notice.

That night the Lord sent the angel of death over the land of Egypt, and every firstborn of the Egyptians died. The death angel "passed over" the Israelites, who were covered and protected by the blood of the lamb smeared on their doorposts. Before that night was over, the Israelites had departed from Egypt, led by Moses and a pillar of fire, signifying the Lord's real and literal presence with them.

No Feeble Ones Among Them

IN ONE NIGHT, God changed the Israelites' entire lifestyle. Their physical conditions and circumstances changed instantly. As it turned out, however, their mindset did not change as quickly. Most Bible scholars believe that there were as many as *four million* Israelites altogether who left Egypt, counting men, women, and children. How was it possible to move such a great host of people all at once?

Consider a modern comparison. What if it was necessary to suddenly evacuate the entire four-million population of a large city? How could we do it? Think for a minute; out of four million people, how many would be in hospitals, in intensive care units, or on heart machines, respirators, or dialysis machines? How many would be confined to their beds at home as complete invalids? How many would need crutches or wheelchairs just to get around? Now think of what would be involved in trying to move these four million people in one night across many miles of wilderness! It would take hundreds of ambulances and thousands of doctors and nurses just to care for the sick and feeble alone! Add to this the fact that everyone was bringing his or her personal belongings, and we begin to grasp a little of the magnitude of such an undertaking.

How did God accomplish it? First of all, when the time came, the Israelites were ready. They had everything packed and ready to roll. A verse from Psalm 105 provides some further insight. "He also brought them out with silver and gold, and there was none feeble among His tribes."[2] None feeble? How could that be? In that one evening, as the Israelites ate the Passover lamb, and had the Passover blood on their doorposts, God released the anointing of the Holy Spirit through the land. On the one hand it spelled judgment for those who rejected the Lord, but on the other hand brought healing, redemption, deliverance, and abundance into the home of every believing Israelite.

I can easily imagine that many of the crippled or sick among Israel at the beginning of that night expected that they would be left behind because they could not handle the trip. Some of them may even have begun to say good-bye to their loved ones. Suddenly, as they partook of that lamb, cripples saw their legs straighten out and become strong; blind people started seeing, and deaf people started hearing. In an instant the Lord healed all the sick and infirm among four million Israelites, because when He led them out, as the psalmist said, "There was none feeble among His tribes."

In addition, the Israelites came out with "silver and gold," the plunder of the Egyptians, who had given riches to the departing Hebrews because God had given His people favor in their sight. God restored to His people everything that had been stolen from them over centuries of slavery, and multiplied it a hundredfold, so that when they departed Egypt, they were one of the richest nations in the entire region. It came into their hands through the power of the Lamb of God.

The lambs that were slaughtered on that first Passover in Egypt, and their blood which was spread on the doorposts of Israelite homes, were a type and a shadow of Jesus Christ, the true Lamb of God who would come one day. His sacrificial death would make forgiveness, healing, and deliverance available for all people. Jesus, the Lamb of God, has the power not only to restore us physically, but also to bring us into abundance. Just as the Israelites were healed physically, delivered from idolatry, and restored financially, Jesus Christ has come to redeem us in every area of life. He doesn't want there to be any feeble among us.

John the Baptist described Jesus as "the Lamb of God who takes away the sin of the world."[3] Whatever our needs are, Jesus can meet them. When we place our faith and trust in Him, not only does He forgive and take away our sin, but He also redeems us from every sickness and breaks every poverty curse. The devil will try to test us, distract us, discourage us, and even destroy us, but we must continue to trust in the power of God and the covering cleansing of Jesus' blood. When we stand on the Word of God, we will see the release of not just natural abundance, but *supernatural* abundance. I believe that we are living in a very prophetic hour in which the Lord is going to transfer the resources of the world into the hands of believing people. The key is the atoning work of the Lamb of God. Just as He delivered Israel from Egypt, He wants to deliver us as individuals, as families, and as the people of God, the Church of the Lord Jesus Christ.

Caught Between the Devil and the Deep Blue Sea

IF THE ISRAELITES THOUGHT that their problems were over as soon as they crossed the border out of Egypt, they were in for a big surprise. Almost as soon as he let them go, Pharaoh changed his mind, summoned his army, and went after them. Often we will find in our own lives that this is the devil's pattern. He will keep chasing us until we cry out, "Lord, is there no rescue?" Sometimes we end up in situations from which there seems to be no escape. This is what happened to Israel. They found themselves with the Red Sea in front of them and Pharaoh's army behind them, ready to consume them.

It's times like these, when our backs are against the wall, that we seem to hear the devil say, "I've got you where I want you; now I'm going to destroy you." If we're not careful, it becomes very easy to blame God for putting us into this kind of position. Then we start complaining, "Oh Lord, why did You bring me here? Why have You abandoned me?" That's what the Israelites did at the Red Sea. They started complaining against God and against Moses for leading them into what appeared to be certain destruction.

I discovered a long time ago that even when things look completely impossible, God always has ten thousand different ways to get us out of it, if we will only look to Him. In Israel's situation, God simply parted the Red Sea and sent His angels to "blow-dry" the sea floor so the Israelites could walk across on dry ground. When the Egyptian army tried to follow, the Lord closed the waters over them and they drowned. Once again, God took a bitter situation and turned it into sweet deliverance. He was trying to build the faith of His people.

Water in the Wilderness

A T THE RED SEA, the Lord turned a time of fear and bitter despair for the Israelites into a time of great joy and celebration. Other great challenges still lay ahead. The first one came only three days after their deliverance at the Red Sea.

So Moses brought Israel from the Red Sea; then they went out into the Wilderness of Shur. And they went three days in the wilderness and found no water. Now when they came to Marah, they could not drink the waters of Marah, for they were bitter. Therefore the name of it was called Marah. And the people complained against Moses, saying, "What shall we drink?" So he cried out to the Lord, and the Lord showed him a tree. When he cast it into the waters, the waters were made sweet. There He made a statute and an ordinance for them, and there He tested them, and said, "If you diligently heed the voice of the Lord your God and do what is right in His sight, give ear to His commandments and keep all His statutes, I will put none of the diseases on you which I have brought on the Egyptians. For I am the Lord who heals you."[4]

The people of Israel followed the Lord and Moses into the wilderness. God had brought them a great deliverance, first from slavery in Egypt, and then from destruction by the Egyptian army. He led them with a pillar of cloud by day and a pillar of fire by night. Finally, after three days in the wilderness without water, the Israelites reached the springs or pools of Marah. They rushed to the water to slake their thirst, only to have found the water bitter and undrinkable.

If you've ever gone three days without water, you will understand how the Israelites felt. I have fasted without water before, and by the third day, I was having visions of giant containers of lemonade! Going without water, either deliberately or involuntarily, really focuses your attention.

God wanted His people to focus their attention on Him and on His ability to provide for them. Remember, this was four million people in the wilderness without water, not to mention all their cattle, sheep, and goats, which also needed water. Was God wrong in the way He led them? Did He say, "Oops, I made a mistake?" No. God deliberately led them where He did in order to test them and teach them to trust Him. Humanly speaking, it may have been an impossible task to provide sufficient water for millions of mouths, but nothing is impossible with God.

I imagine that God was disappointed—but not surprised—by the response of the people. Instead of turning their minds back to how the Lord had delivered them out of Egypt and across the Red Sea, and then trusting Him to provide for them now, they began complaining bitterly to Moses. The Israelites were now free people, but they still thought like slaves. For generations, theirs had been a hand-to-mouth, hardscrabble existence—a daily struggle just to survive. They had very limited vision, which had not been broadened even by all the miracles they had seen. A slave mentality dies hard.

Apparently, Moses was the only one who had the faith and good sense not to complain, but rather to appeal to the Lord instead. As Moses sought God, God showed him a tree which, when cast into the bitter water, turned the water sweet. God performed a great miracle: He turned a bitter pool into sweet water so that a host of four million people could drink and be revived and refreshed.

Moses heard God's Word and he acted on it. His simple act of faith and obedience released the miracle power of God; the whole pool

143

became sweet, and millions of people were able to drink. A simple act of faith brought God's healing to their bitter pool.

It was in the wake of this great miracle that God revealed Himself to His people in a new way. He said, "I am *'Jehovah-Rapha'*—the Lord who heals you." From this point on, the Israelites would know God in a way they had never known Him before. Healing is part of God's nature; He doesn't even have to think about it. Speaking through the prophet Malachi, God said, "For I am the Lord, I do not change."[5] Since He does not change, who God was for Israel then, He is for us today; what He did for Israel then, He will do for us today. Yesterday, today, and forever, God is *Jehovah-Rapha*, the Lord who heals us.

Everyone Has a Bitter Pool

ONE INESCAPABLE PRINCIPLE OR REALITY OF LIFE is that all of us have to go by a bitter pool at one time or another. It may be a dreadfully sick child, a painful marriage, separation or divorce, financial reversal, business failure, betrayal by a trusted friend—anything. Whatever our bitter pool may be, it is important that we learn from it.

Our temptation is to act just like the children of Israel who, stuck in their slave mentality, murmured and complained and rebelled against the Lord until, ultimately, they were condemned to wander in the wilderness for 40 years instead of entering the Promised Land as God had intended. The Israelites acted like slaves instead of like sons and daughters of God. The danger is that we could do the same when we come to our bitter pool. God does not want us to act like slaves, but like His sons and daughters. We have been redeemed by the blood of the Lamb, and we need to behave like redeemed people. When we do—when we walk and live by faith in our Lord no matter what our circumstances—we will begin to see His provision and healing for ourselves.

Sometimes God will call us to praise Him and thank Him in the midst of our bitter pool—*before* deliverance or healing comes. Sometimes He will ask us to give in the middle of difficult circumstances, or remain cheerful and confident in the face of tremendous trials. This is when our faith proves itself. Do you have a great need in your life? Are you willing to trust and follow the Lord completely even *before* He meets that need? Do you need to be healed? Are you willing to acknowledge Christ as Lord and follow Him faithfully even if He *never* heals you? Bitter pools test our faith.

In obedience to God's command, Moses threw the tree into the bitter waters of Marah, and the entire pool was healed. In the Bible, water is often used as a symbol for a nation or a people. Here, the water is healed by a tree. That tree was a type, or a symbol of the cross upon which Jesus would die and thereby bring healing to the nations. The cross was Jesus' bitter pool, and because of it, all of our bitter pools can be healed. I can say with complete confidence and with no apology that because of what Jesus Christ did on Calvary for you and me, He can heal every bitter pool.

All it takes is a simple act of faith to release God's miracle power and healing anointing. Many times I have had people write to me, saying simply, "Brother Mahesh, we need a miracle of healing for so-and-so. Please pray for us." I pray over every letter I receive, but sometimes when I am traveling I do not see these requests until several weeks after they were written. There have been several occasions in which I have not had a chance to pray over a situation, yet receive another letter saying, "Thank you for praying; we got our miracle." It was their simple act of faith in writing to me, not my prayers, that released the miracle. It was their trust in God and His power, not their confidence in me, that brought them the victory.

God Uses Bitter Pools to Reveal Himself to Us

OUR GOD IS A GOD OF REVELATION. He is always revealing Himself; otherwise, we could never come to know Him. To Abraham, God revealed Himself as "Jehovah-Jireh," the Lord our Provider. Once Abraham came to know God that way, that knowledge and that revelation were his personal possession forever. That's why, when the king of Sodom sought to give Abraham silver and gold and riches in return for his help in a battle, Abraham refused, saying, "I don't need your money. The Lord is my provider."[6]

145

God as Provider has become a living truth for me over the years. I love to give away, because I know that God is my provider. Jesus said, "Give, and it will be given to you: good measure, pressed down, shaken together, and running over will be put into your bosom. For with the same measure that you use, it will be measured back to you."[7] That's the kind of God we have!

At the waters of Marah, God revealed Himself as "Jehovah-Rapha," the Lord our Healer. As the Israelites understood that and believed it, that revelation and knowledge became part of their equipment as a people; it became their personal possession. That's the same way God wants it to be with each of us. He wants the revelation of Himself as our healer to become our personal and permanent possession, not just for ourselves individually, but also for our families, our churches, and our nations.

God brings us by bitter pools in order to give us a greater revelation of Himself, so that in that revelation, our greater knowledge of Him can become our own personal possession. If He does not lead us to bitter pools and through difficult times, there is no way that we can truly know or understand His greatness, and we can never possess Him that way. When God reveals Himself to us, particularly through a "bitter pool" experience, it's as if scales fall off our eyes, and we see a truth for the very first time. That truth about God becomes a part of us. We absorb it like a sponge, and once it is inside of us, no one can take it away. When God's revelations become a living part of us, they change us completely.

When Bitter Pools Come, Look to See What God Is Doing

BACK IN CHAPTER FOUR I related the difficulties and heartache that surrounded the premature birth of our son Aaron. At the time, both my wife, Bonnie, and Aaron were in serious trouble. This was a bitter, bitter pool that God brought us to. As we listened to the litany of problems—our son was dying, his brain was hemorrhaging, if he lived he would be a vegetable, his lungs had not formed completely, and large portions of his intestines were dead—sorrow piled upon sorrow and pain upon pain. Watching Aaron's tiny chest move slightly with every labored breath, any one of which could be his last, tore at our hearts. It was a bitter pool.

Turning Bitter Water Into Sweet

As people who had long since given our lives to Jesus and had already seen thousands come to the Lord through our ministry, it would have been very easy and tempting for us to murmur and complain. Instead, we chose to look to God and say, "Lord, we belong to You. We love You and trust You, and release Aaron and this whole situation into Your hands."

I left for Africa, never expecting to see Aaron alive again. Yet, it was during that trip that God chose to reveal Himself to me and to thousands of Africans in an awesome and powerful way by raising six-year-old Katshinyi from the dead. I returned home to find Aaron healed and whole. God had turned our bitter pool (not to mention the bitter pool of Katshinyi's family) into sweet water, and in so doing revealed Himself to us as the Resurrection and the Life. It was a revelation that will stay with me forever, as well as with everyone who witnessed it or was a part of it. God brought us through a bitter pool in order to bring greater glory to His name.

Whenever you come to a bitter pool in your life, don't let the devil lie to you and make you think that your problems are because you've done something wrong. Remember that the devil is the accuser of the brethren. Instead of feeling guilty, or murmuring and complaining, recognize your bitter pool as an opportunity for God to reveal and glorify Himself in your life and circumstances. When these tough times come, look around you, alert to see what God is doing. If you are seeking to trust and obey Him, in His time He will turn your bitter pool into an abundant, bubbling spring of great joy and blessing.

God uses the crucible of suffering and bitter pools to forge, fashion, and temper a great army of saints who have been broken and then healed, and made sensitive to His heart of compassion for the broken, sick, and hurting people of the world. He is calling us to let Him turn our bitter pools into sweet water, so that He can then use us as His instruments in healing the bitter pools of people everywhere. The pain of our own bitter pools sensitizes us to the pain of others, so that we can better feel the pulse of God's heart, see His purpose more clearly, and understand our calling more fully. Having our bitter pools transformed into sweet water

147

by the power of God helps us to grow in faith and trust so that we will commit ourselves to *obeying our heavenly vision.*

Endnotes

1. 2 Kings 2:19-22.

2. Ps. 105:37.

3. Jn. 1:29b.

4. Ex. 15:22-26.

5. Mal. 3:6a.

6. See Gen. 14:22-24, paraphrased.

7. Lk. 6:38.

Chapter Ten

Obeying Our Heavenly Vision

YEARS AGO, WHEN I WORKED IN TEXAS at a state school for mentally retarded children, I split my time between the girls' dormitory, which was called "Rose," and the boys' dormitory, which was called "Lily." I usually spent my mornings in "Rose," heading up behavior modification programs for the girls, and my afternoons in "Lily," working with the boys.

One afternoon I had finished my work in "Rose" and had gone to "Lily" to work with the boys when I felt the Holy Spirit say to me very gently, "Go back to Rose." It was a pretty clear nudging, but I was trying to be reasonable and practical, so I said, "No, I've already been there today." Again I heard the gentle but persistent voice, "Go back to Rose." I tried to ignore it by busying myself with other things. Some time went by and then the voice returned. "Go back to Rose."

I was young in the ministry at the time and still had *a lot* to learn about following the Lord! I protested, "Lord, I was there all morning! Why should I go back? It just isn't logical." Have you ever argued with the Lord, or found yourself trying to "explain" to Him why something He says isn't logical? "Lord, You just don't understand..." or "Lord, You just don't know *my* situation!" I know better than that now, but back then I could sometimes be a little thickheaded.

The Hidden Power of the Believer's Touch

Despite my arguing, the patient, gentle voice of the Spirit would not leave me alone. Eventually I said, "All right! I don't know why, but I'll go back to Rose!" I closed my office in "Lily" and walked back to the girls' dormitory. When I got there, I walked right into the middle of an emergency situation. The school conducted a foster grandparents program in which senior citizens could take some of the children out for walks or just spend some time with them. A 14-year-old mute girl named Helen had been out for a walk with one of the seniors in the program. Upon returning Helen to the dormitory, this elderly individual had inadvertently put Helen in the wrong room, an isolation room with a door that could not be opened from the inside. It was used for securing someone who had become out of control. At the time Helen was left there accidentally, the room was already occupied by a very large and profoundly mentally handicapped girl who was in a total frenzy. This girl took her boots and started beating Helen repeatedly in the face. Being mute, Helen could not even cry out for help. She was a gentle and precious little girl, and was completely helpless against the bigger girl's attack.

When I walked into "Rose" that afternoon, the staff had just found Helen. Her face was all purple and black and swollen, except for her eyes, which were filled with huge tears. The nurses and attendants were there, but I knew then that the Holy Spirit had sent me to help Helen. I sat down beside her, held her hand, and touched her forehead, and said, "Helen, Jesus loves you, and I love you, too." Something that felt like sparks shot from my hand to hers, and within the space of two minutes, Helen's bruised face turned from purple and black to dark red, then to pink, and then to normal! In two minutes, the Lord healed Helen right on the spot!

At this time in my life, the Lord had already begun to move me in the direction of a healing ministry, and in fact, used me on numerous occasions to bring healing among some of the children there at the state school. If I had ignored the Spirit's prompting that day, what would have happened to Helen? Would the Lord have healed her anyway? Perhaps. He certainly didn't *need* me in order to do it, but one of the truly amazing things about God is that He *chooses* to use ordinary, flawed human beings to accomplish His will and purpose. From my perspective, if I had failed to heed the Spirit's voice, I would have been unfaithful to His call on my life. I would have *disobeyed my heavenly vision.*

Seeing Eye-to-Eye With God

GOD HAS A WAY SOMETIMES of stepping into our lives, stopping us dead in our tracks, and by imparting to us *His* vision and anointing, setting us off in a totally new direction. This is exactly what happened to the apostle Paul one day on the road to Damascus, and it changed him and the focus of his life forever. Once, while in custody because of accusations lodged against him by some of his enemies, Paul defended himself before Festus, the Roman procurator of Judea, and Agrippa, the Roman-approved king of Palestine. In his testimony, Paul shared plainly and boldly how God had stepped in and changed his life. He began by telling of his early zeal as a persecutor of the Church and how he hunted down Christians wherever he could find them.

> *While thus occupied, as I journeyed to Damascus with authority and commission from the chief priests, at midday, O king, along the road I saw a light from heaven, brighter than the sun, shining around me and those who journeyed with me. And when we all had fallen to the ground, I heard a voice speaking to me and saying in the Hebrew language, "Saul, Saul, why are you persecuting Me? It is hard for you to kick against the goads." So I said, "Who are You, Lord?" And He said, "I am Jesus, whom you are persecuting. But rise and stand on your feet; for I have appeared to you for this purpose, to make you a minister and a witness both of the things which you have seen and of the things which I will yet reveal to you. I will deliver you from the Jewish people, as well as from the Gentiles, to whom I now send you, to open their eyes, in order to turn them from darkness to light, and from the power of satan to God, that they may receive forgiveness of sins and an inheritance among those who are sanctified by faith in Me." Therefore, King Agrippa, I was not disobedient to the heavenly vision, but declared first to those in Damascus and in Jerusalem, and throughout all the region of Judea, and then to the Gentiles,*

151

that they should repent, turn to God, and do works befitting repentance.[1]

Look again at Paul's words, "I was not disobedient to the heavenly vision...." What vision was that? It was the vision that Jesus gave him when He said that Paul would be "a minister and a witness both of the things which you have *seen* and of the things which *I will yet reveal to you.*" When Paul got in a position where he could finally see eye-to-eye with God, he was never again the same.

Proud, arrogant Paul had to be humbled in the dust of the Damascus road before he could really see God and catch the heavenly vision. The brightness of the *Shekinah* glory of the Lord, brighter than the sun, knocked Paul right off his donkey. There, with dirt on his face and scales on his eyes, he encountered the risen Savior. Paul started out going in one direction and ended up headed in another. He still went to Damascus as he had planned, but his agenda had changed. The Lord blinded him temporarily, but at the same time gave him a vision that included a divine assignment and a holy calling and destiny: to open the eyes of Jews and Gentiles alike, to turn them from spiritual darkness to God's holy light, and from the power of satan to God.

When the Lord gives us an assignment or a vision, He rarely tells us everything up front. He expects us to follow Him and trust Him to reveal certain things later on. It's almost as though He presents us with a blank contract and says, "Sign here." When we protest and say, "But Lord, this is *blank*," He says, "I know. I'll fill in the details later. Sign here."

Paul signed. He was obedient to his heavenly vision, and paid a heavy price for it: beatings, stonings, shipwrecks, imprisonment, and hardship and privations of every kind. Paul's vision drove him with a consuming passion. At one point he wrote, "For if I preach the gospel, I have nothing to boast of, for necessity is laid upon me; yes, woe is me if I do not preach the gospel!"[2]

Was it worth it? Did Paul ever have any regrets about being true to his heavenly vision? Absolutely not. "But what things were gain to me, these I have counted loss for Christ. Yet indeed I also count all things loss for the excellence of the knowledge of Christ Jesus my Lord, for whom I have suffered the loss of all things, and count them as rubbish, that I may gain Christ and be found in Him...."³ "For I am already being poured out as a drink offering, and the time of my departure is at hand. I have fought the good fight, I have finished the race, I have kept the faith. Finally, there is laid up for me the crown of righteousness, which the Lord, the righteous Judge, will give to me on that Day."⁴ Paul came to see eye-to-eye with God, and everything else paled in comparison. He caught the heavenly vision, and he liked the view.

Heavenly Vision Comes With a Price

PAUL WAS NEVER UNDER ANY ILLUSIONS that obeying his heavenly vision would be easy. Aside from the physical hardships he endured, there was the constant tension of opposition from enemies and the heartache of being misunderstood by believers and unbelievers alike. During his defense before Festus and Agrippa, Paul boldly declared the gospel of Jesus:

> *"Therefore, having obtained help from God, to this day I stand, witnessing both to small and great, saying no other things than those which the prophets and Moses said would come—that the Christ would suffer, that He would be the first to rise from the dead, and would proclaim light to the Jewish people and to the Gentiles." Now as he thus made his defense, Festus said with a loud voice, "Paul, you are beside yourself! Much learning is driving you mad!" But he said, "I am not mad, most noble Festus, but speak the words of truth and reason."*⁵

When Festus heard Paul declare that Jesus had risen from the dead, he thought the apostle had lost his mind. Whenever we commit to obey our heavenly vision, we have to accept the reality that some people will think we are crazy. What may be even harder to bear is the fact that some of our friends and family—people we love and care about deeply—will misunderstand. They will try to talk us out of it or convince us that we have made a mistake. They're not our enemies; they simply don't understand. Satan, however, may try to launch all sorts of physical and mental attacks to wear us down and distract us. The physical, emotional, and psychological pressures can become so great that we can break down and give up unless we are rock-solid concerning our call and absolutely clear-eyed with regard to our heavenly vision.

That's why it is so important that we have no doubts about our call from the Lord to walk in the healing anointing in this end-time generation. Sometimes it is hard to clear away the boulder of doubt that blocks our way on the road of faith. In this regard, James gives us wise counsel, along with a caution: "If any of you lacks wisdom, let him ask of God, who gives to all liberally and without reproach, and it will be given to him. But let him ask in faith, with no doubting, for he who doubts is like a wave of the sea driven and tossed by the wind. For let not that man suppose that he will receive anything from the Lord."[6] If you need wisdom, pray; if you have doubts, pray. The Lord will give the one, and take away the other.

We have to discern and recognize our heavenly vision before we can obey it. How do we do this? Remember the triad of truths upon which we stand: the living Word of God ("Faith comes by hearing, and hearing by the Word of God"[7]), the finished work of Christ ("For I determined not to know anything among you except Jesus Christ and Him crucified"[8]), and the indwelling presence of the Holy Spirit ("I will put My Spirit in you, and you shall live..."[9]). When we know and stand on the Word of God, when we know and nurture a love relationship with our risen Savior, and when we know and welcome the Person of the Holy Spirit, we are in the proper spiritual position to receive and recognize our heavenly vision.

God Is Still in the Healing Business

I BELIEVE THAT GOD HAS A VISION FOR EVERY BELIEVER. I also believe that in this end-time generation He is raising up an army of anointed servants who will walk in the miracle dimension of healing, signs, and wonders. It is my firm conviction that any believer who is willing to pay the price and pursue this heavenly vision can walk in the healing anointing. God is still healing today, just as He always has, and He is looking for people who are willing to be His instruments for dispensing healing to the nations.

*****

In October 1991, an 11-year-old boy from Spain named David attended our healing service in Jerusalem with his family. David was born with spina bifida. A gymnastics accident had hospitalized him, and x-rays clearly revealed the missing bone in his spine. Doctors told David that permanent paralysis would result and that after he stopped growing, a bone graft would be necessary. David received prayer for healing, and subsequent x-rays in November showed that God had miraculously put vertebrae where there had been none before! David and his family returned to Jerusalem the following year and shared their story with me and showed me the x-rays of David's completely healed spine. *God is still in the healing business!*

*****

In December 1991, a nine-year-old girl named Laura began complaining of earaches. Her doctor treated her with an antibiotic for an ear infection. Laura also suffered from severe chronic asthma and was susceptible to upper respiratory infections. The medicine cleared up her ear infection, but then she began complaining that she could not hear very well.

A series of thorough tests by an audiologist determined that Laura had suffered major permanent hearing loss and required hearing aids for both ears. Her parents ordered the hearing aids and Laura began wearing them in early April 1992.

Late that same month, Laura and her parents, who are officers in the Salvation Army, attended one of my meetings in Ohio. When I called out for the parents and their daughter who had asthma, Laura came forward for prayer. When I laid hands on her, she fell under the Spirit. As Laura herself described what happened, "All of a sudden I just sorta felt this 'zap' in my body. It started at my head and went to my ears. I started to hear ringing in my ears, then there was a sort-of tickling through my body and in my chest, and then I started feeling really terrific with my asthma and my ears."

The Hidden Power of the Believer's Touch

Laura's hearing was fully restored that night. She went home insisting to her parents that she no longer needed her hearing aids. Subsequent tests the following month at the audiologist confirmed that there was no trace of any hearing loss! *God is still in the healing business!*

*****

In 1997, during a miracle service in Sunderland, England, a young woman named Julie was healed of an arm injury. A year before, the bone in her upper right arm had shattered, severing the radial nerves. She was admitted to the hospital where doctors grafted some bone from her hip into her arm. Julie could not raise her arm, and she was told that she would never regain full use of it.

During our miracle service, the Lord recreated the radial nerves in her arm! She gave public testimony at the meeting, demonstrating her healing by showing full range of motion and usage of her arm. The doctor who had admitted her to the hospital the year before was also present at the meeting, and confirmed Julie's healing. *God is still in the healing business!*

*****

In 1998, a woman called "J. F." attended one of our Watch of the Lord conferences, shortly after receiving a medical report from her doctor confirming that she had Lupus. She was completely healed during the Friday afternoon conference session. As "J. F." shared in her testimony,

I was sitting in my seat praying, "I need a healing and I need to hear Mahesh pray for Lupus." Just as I prayed that prayer, Mahesh called out, "Lupus." I rushed forward and Mahesh prayed for me. I could feel the burning, healing touch of the Lord go through me. After the conference I went back to the doctor to be checked regarding the type of Lupus. The doctor responded with a puzzled look on her face and said, "You do not have Lupus. I don't understand." I told her, "The Lord healed me!" *God is still in the healing business!*

*****

156

In November 1999, a woman named Darlene and her family from the West Central Highlands of Virginia attended a Waves of Glory Conference at our church in Charlotte, North Carolina. By their own words, they went away with "cups overflowing." They had just gotten home and started to unpack when a sister-in-law named Phyllis drove up. Phyllis suffered from severe asthma and had also been diagnosed with an incurable, degenerative condition known as Chronic Obstructive Pulmonary Disease, or COPD. This disease prevents the lungs from receiving and channeling sufficient amounts of oxygen to the blood, and thus affects the heart, lungs, and other vital organs. The lungs gradually cease to function, leading to a slow, suffocating death. Phyllis was slowly dying, and there was nothing anyone could do.

Phyllis arrived at Darlene's house in the throes of a severe asthma attack. Darlene saw that Phyllis was laboring to breathe, and knew something had to be done immediately. Without hesitating, Darlene laid her hand on Phyllis' chest and began praying for God's help. Suddenly and without warning, Phyllis fell backwards to the floor under the power of God, where she remained for 15 or 20 minutes. While on the floor, she had a vision of Jesus. When she rose, everyone discovered that all the amalgam fillings in her teeth had been changed to a gold-like substance! This was a sovereign display of God's glory and blessing. More important, however, is that Phyllis' lungs were completely healed, and remain so today! Her dentist has confirmed the change in her fillings, and her family doctor, the healing of her asthma and COPD. *God is still in the healing business!*

Will You Take the Plunge?

THE TESTIMONY OF DARLENE AND PHYLLIS is a perfect illustration of how God can and does use "ordinary folk" to carry His healing anointing. God has a purpose and a calling for every life, yours as well as mine. He has a vision for each of us. I hope and pray that we all will be able to stand before the Lord one day and affirm as Paul did that we were not disobedient to the heavenly vision. Can we be disobedient? Yes, we can. The choice is completely ours. Disobedience means grieving the Holy Spirit and missing out on the fullest joy and blessings that come with unreserved surrender of our lives to the lordship of Christ.

The Hidden Power of the Believer's Touch

Because Paul obeyed his heavenly vision, today literally millions of people around the world read the words he wrote under the Spirit's inspiration, and come into a saving relationship with Christ through repentance and faith. Millions more who are already believers are formed into mature, growing disciples through the words of this man who was one of the greatest intellects of his day. Yet, Paul humbled himself completely before the King of glory. Through Paul as much as through any other single individual, the Lord transformed the first-century world. It was because Paul obeyed his heavenly vision.

Christ is calling us, His end-time Bride, to be obedient to our heavenly vision. We must humble ourselves, seek His face, and say, "Lord, I will obey. I will be true to my heavenly vision." It's time to step out of the boat and plunge into the rushing river that flows from the throne and the heart of God. It is a river of the Spirit, carrying us to the sick and the dying, the hurting and the hungry. Our marching orders are the same as those of our Master:

The Spirit of the Lord is upon Me,
Because He has anointed Me
To preach the gospel to the poor;
He has sent Me to heal the brokenhearted,
To proclaim liberty to the captives
And recovery of sight to the blind,
To set at liberty those who are oppressed;
To proclaim the acceptable year of the Lord.[10]

The apostle John, while in the Spirit on the island of Patmos, received a beautiful vision of the river of God which foreshadows the glory that is to come:

And he showed me a pure river of water of life, clear as crystal, proceeding from the throne of God and of the Lamb. In the middle of its street, and on either side of the river, was the tree of life, which bore twelve fruits, each tree yielding its fruit every month. The leaves of the tree were for the healing of the nations. And there shall be no more curse, but the throne of God and of the Lamb shall be in it, and His servants shall serve Him.[11]

Healing has come! The curse is broken! The dwelling place of the Lord is in the midst of His people, and all the nations will be glad! The earth will be filled with the glory of God as the waters cover the sea!

The living waters of the river of God issue forth from the hearts and lives of His people. Let's listen, believe, and pay heed to the words of Jesus, who said,

If anyone thirsts, let him come to Me and drink. He who believes in Me, as the Scripture has said, out of his heart will flow rivers of living water.[12]

Let go! Plunge into the water and let the current of the Spirit carry you into the miracle dimension of healings, signs, and wonders. Let your life be a channel for the outflow of God's abundant rivers of living water! Let Him use you to touch others with its life-giving flow! *Life grows where the river flows!*

Endnotes

1. Acts 26:12-20.
2. 1 Cor. 9:16.
3. Phil. 3:7-9a.
4. 2 Tim. 4:6-8a.
5. Acts 26:22-25.
6. Jas. 1:5-7.
7. Rom. 10:17.
8. 1 Cor. 2:2.
9. Ezek. 37:14a.
10. Lk. 4:18-19.
11. Rev. 22:1-3.
12. Jn. 7:37b-38.

For other books, audiotapes, or other resource material from the author, contact:

Mahesh Chavda Ministries International
P.O. Box 411008
Charlotte, NC 28241
(707) 543-7272
FAX: (704) 541-5300

E-mail: info@watchofthelord.com

www.watchofthelord.com

Foundationally Spirit-filled. Biblically Sound. Spiritually Inspirational.

━━ THE LOST ART OF INTERCESSION
by Jim W. Goll.
Finally there is something that really explains what is happening to so many folk in the Body of Christ. What does it mean to carry the burden of the Lord? Where is it in Scripture and in history? Why do I feel as though God is groaning within me? No, you are not crazy; God is restoring genuine intercessory prayer in the hearts of those who are open to respond to His burden and His passion.
ISBN 1-56043-697-2

━━ FATHER, FORGIVE US!
by Jim W. Goll.
What is holding back a worldwide "great awakening"? What hinders the Church all over the world from rising up and bringing in the greatest harvest ever known? The answer is simple: sin! God is calling Christians today to take up the mantle of identificational intercession and repent for the sins of the present and past; for the sins of our fathers; for the sins of the nations. Will you heed the call? This book shows you how!
ISBN 0-7684-2025-3

━━ THE HIDDEN POWER OF PRAYER AND FASTING
by Mahesh Chavda.
The praying believer is the confident believer. But the fasting believer is the overcoming believer. This is the believer who changes the circumstances and the world around him. He is the one who experiences the supernatural power of the risen Lord in his everyday life. An international evangelist and the senior pastor of All Nations Church in Charlotte, North Carolina, Mahesh Chavda has seen firsthand the power of God released through a lifestyle of prayer and fasting. Here he shares from decades of personal experience and scriptural study principles and practical tips about fasting and praying. This book will inspire you to tap into God's power and change your life, your city, and your nation!
ISBN 0-7684-2017-2

━━ ENCOUNTERING THE PRESENCE
by Colin Urquhart.
What is it about Jesus that, when we encounter Him, we are changed? When we encounter the Presence, we encounter the Truth, because Jesus is the Truth. Here Colin Urquhart, best-selling author and pastor in Sussex, England, explains how the Truth changes facts. Do you desire to become more like Jesus? The Truth will set you free!
ISBN 0-7684-2018-0

Available at your local Christian bookstore.

For more information and sample chapters, visit www.reapernet.com

6B-2:64

*T*itles that will challenge & encourage you!

─── **SECRET SOURCES OF POWER**

by T.F. Tenney with Tommy Tenney.

Everyone is searching for power. People are longing for some external force to empower their lives and transform their circumstances. *Secret Sources of Power* furnishes some of the keys that will unlock the door to Divine power. You might be surprised at what is on the other side of that door. It will be the opposite of the world's concepts of power and how to obtain it. You will discover that before you lay hold of God's power you must let go of your own resources. You will be challenged to go down before you can be lifted up. Death always comes before resurrection. If you are dissatisfied with your life and long for the power of God to be manifested in you then now is the time. Take the keys and open the door to *Secret Sources of Power*!

ISBN 0-7684-5000-4

─── **THE GOD CHASERS** (National Best-Seller)

by Tommy Tenney.

There are those so hungry, so desperate for His presence, that they become consumed with finding Him. Their longing for Him moves them to do what they would otherwise never do: Chase God. But what does it really mean to chase God? Can He be "caught"? Is there an end to the thirsting of man's soul for Him? Meet Tommy Tenney—God chaser. Join him in his search for God. Follow him as he ignores the maze of religious tradition and finds himself, not chasing God, but to his utter amazement, caught by the One he had chased.

ISBN 0-7684-2016-4

Also available in Spanish

ISBN 0-7899-0642-2

─── **GOD CHASERS DAILY MEDITATION & PERSONAL JOURNAL**

by Tommy Tenney.

ISBN 0-7684-2040-7

─── **THE POWER OF BROKENNESS**

by Don Nori.

Accepting Brokenness is a must for becoming a true vessel of the Lord, and is a stepping-stone to revival in our hearts, our homes, and our churches. Brokenness alone brings us to the wonderful revelation of how deep and great our Lord's mercy really is. Join this companion who leads us through the darkest of nights. Discover the *Power of Brokenness*.

ISBN 1-56043-178-4

─── **SECRETS OF THE MOST HOLY PLACE**

by Don Nori.

Here is a prophetic parable you will read again and again. The winds of God are blowing, drawing you to His Life within the Veil of the Most Holy Place. There you begin to see as you experience a depth of relationship your heart has yearned for. This book is a living, dynamic experience with God!

ISBN 1-56043-076-1

Available at your local Christian bookstore.

For more information and sample chapters, visit www.reapernet.com

6B-2:53

Exciting titles
by Dr. Bill Hamon

━ APOSTLES, PROPHETS AND THE COMING MOVES OF GOD

Author of the "Prophets" series, Dr. Bill Hamon brings the same anointed instruction in this new series on apostles! Learn about the apostolic age and how apostles and prophets work together. Find out God's end-time plans for the Church!
ISBN 0-939868-09-1

━ PROPHETS AND PERSONAL PROPHECY

This book defines the role of a prophet or prophetess and gives the reader strategic guidelines for judging prophecy. Many of the stories included are taken from Dr. Bill's ministry and add that "hands on" practicality that is quickly making this book a best-seller.
ISBN 0-939868-03-2

━ PROPHETS AND THE PROPHETIC MOVEMENT

This sequel to *Prophets and Personal Prophecy* is packed with the same kind of cutting instruction that made the first volume a best-seller. Prophetic insights, how-to's, and warnings make this book essential for the Spirit-filled church.
ISBN 0-939868-04-0

━ PROPHETS, PITFALLS, AND PRINCIPLES

This book shows you how to recognize your hidden "root" problems, and detect and correct character flaws and "weed seed" attitudes. It also can teach you how to discern true prophets using Dr. Hamon's ten M's.
ISBN 0-939868-05-9

6B-1:19

More titles
by Mark Hanby

➤ YOU HAVE NOT MANY FATHERS

"My son, give me your heart." So says the proverb, echoing the heart and passion of our Father in Heaven. God has spiritual "dads" all over the world whom He has filled with wisdom, knowledge, compassion, and most of all, love for those young in the faith. You do not have to go through your life untrained and unloved; uncared for and forgotten. There are fathers in Christ who are waiting to pour all they have into your heart, as Elijah did for Elisha. "My son, give me your heart."
ISBN 1-56043-166-0

➤ YOU HAVE NOT MANY FATHERS STUDY GUIDE

ISBN 0-7684-2036-9

➤ THE HOUSE THAT GOD BUILT

Beyond whatever man can desire is a God-given pattern for the life of the Church. Here Dr. Hanby unfolds practical applications from the design of the Tabernacle that allow us to become the house God is building today.
ISBN 1-56043-091-5

➤ THE HOUSE THAT GOD BUILT STUDY GUIDE

ISBN 0-7684-2048-2

➤ THE RENEWING OF THE HOLY GHOST

Do you need renewal? Everything in the natural, from birds to blood cells, must either undergo a process of renewal or enter into death. Our spiritual life is no different. With this book, your renewal can begin today!
ISBN 1-56043-031-1

➤ ANOINTING THE UNSANCTIFIED

The anointing is more than a talented performance or an emotional response. In this book, Dr. Hanby details the essential ingredients of directional relationship that allow the Spirit of God to flow down upon the Body of Christ—and from us to the needs of a dying world.
ISBN 1-56043-071-0

➤ PERCEIVING THE WHEEL OF GOD

On the potter's wheel, a lump of clay yields to a necessary process of careful pressure and constant twisting. Similarly, the form of true faith is shaped by a trusting response to God in a suffering situation. This book offers essential understanding for victory through the struggles of life.
ISBN 1-56043-109-1

Available at your local Christian bookstore.